A PRACTICAL GUIDE TO HUNTING

A Practical Guide to Hunting

Anne Holland

The Crowood Press

First published in 1990 by
The Crowood Press Ltd
Gipsy Lane, Swindon,
Wiltshire SN2 6DQ

British Library Cataloguing in Publication Data

Holland, Anne
　　A practical guide to hunting.
　　1.　Great Britain. Foxes. Hunting
　　I.　Title
　　799.25974442

　　ISBN 1 85223 255 2

To my father, Rex Holland, and to fox-hunters everywhere.

Throughout this book the pronouns 'he', 'him' and 'his' have
been used inclusively and are intended to apply to both males and
females, be they human or equine.

The author wishes to express her thanks to the following for
permission to reproduce their photographs in this book:
Jim Meads (Figs 1, 2, 3, 4, 5, 22, 25, 32, 42, 51, 53, 59, 60, 61,
66, 67, 68, 70, 72, 73, 74, 75, 76, 77, 78, 85, 90); Kevill
Armstrong (Figs 6, 14, 15, 17, 19, 24, 28, 45, 49); Maggie
Rawlinson (Figs 7, 8, 9, 10, 12, 13, 18, 20, 21, 23, 26, 29, 30,
34, 35, 36, 37, 38, 39, 40, 41, 43, 44, 46, 50, 54, 55, 56, 57,
58, 62, 63, 65, 69, 71, 79, 80, 81, 82, 83, 84, 86, 87, 88, 89, 92)
and Ted Walsh (Figs 27, 47, 48, 52, 64, 91).

Typeset by Alacrity Phototypesetting, Banwell Castle,
Weston-super-Mare, Avon.
Printed and bound in Great Britain by BPCC Hazell Books Ltd,
Aylesbury.

Contents

Preface

How fortunate I consider myself that, when learning to ride, I never had to suffer the tedium of trotting around in boring circles. Instead, lessons were hacks in the woods and forestry, miles and miles of it, with bracken pony high, silver birch trees, beautiful beeches, little glades and streams. Hunting was then a natural progression. We were taught as we rode along: heels down, toes up, elbows in and grip with your knees. To encourage us to master the latter, we had to put a leaf between each knee and pretend it was a five pound note (or was it a one pound note?) Anyway, it was certainly big money to a seven or eight year old in those days.

Now, I believe, this is out of fashion, so does it really matter whether or not there has ever been formal tuition with exams taken and letters after my name? In this guide to hunting for the newcomer, not all the tips are 'according to the book' but are gleaned from practical experience in the field. My advice that follows on riding to hounds is spoken from more than thirty happy seasons' hunting, and my aim is simply to help newcomers derive as much pleasure from this wonderful country sport as I have over the years, and hope to for many more to come.

My thanks go to Brian Toon and Anthony Hart of the Masters of Foxhounds Association; to the indefatigable hunting photographer Jim Meads, and to all those who have given their help and support for this guide.

Anne Holland

1 How to Start

'I would like to take up hunting but I'm afraid of making a fool of myself.' How many would-be riders to hounds or fox-hunters (not huntsmen as the only *huntsman* is the man with the horn) have uttered that plea? Fortunately, for those who have gone ahead and tried it anyway, they soon discover there is an *esprit de corps* in the hunting field, in which the newcomer is welcomed, encouraged and guided. There is no need whatsoever to be able to jump large fences. The would-be follower has probably heard awesome stories of derring-do and feats accomplished. It is a little like the fisherman boasting, with the fish he has caught growing in quantity and size with every telling, usually over a pint or two.

Some countries (the hunting parlance for the area covered by each individual hunt has nothing to do with national borders) are well fenced, but there is almost invariably a way round, while other hunts, such as on moorland, have

Fig 1 Cub-hunting. The South Devon Hunt meeting at Hound Tor, near Widecombe on Dartmoor.

Fig 2   The Cattistock Hunt in Dorset.

hardly any jumping, yet the hunting can be just as thrilling. One of the best days I ever had was with the Spooners and West Dartmoor, seven miles over the moor at flying pace where fences would only have got in the way.

As with any sport, the more one knows about it, the more it can be enjoyed. It is preferable to go out with as much understanding of what is going on as possible and with an awareness of the basic etiquette, and then it will not matter at all being a novice rider. In many ways, hunting is like a large club with all the camaraderie that goes with it and, for many, the social aspect is all. For others it is simply the riding and for some it is the actual art of hunting, but for all, nothing can match the tingling anticipation at the start of a hunt and the sense of well-being at the end.

First Approaches

The most likely way to find out about the local hunt is from friends who already belong, or through the Pony Club if you have a child who is a member. It is often through ponies and children that adults take up riding and hunting at a mature age. Conversely, many children who hunt are from non-horsey backgrounds who, therefore, have not grown up to the traditions. For them, too, it is equally important to find out all they can before they start.

The first person to contact about hunting is the local hunt Secretary. If you do not know his or her name, or even the name of the local hunt, try telephoning the local paper. Failing that, telephone *Horse and Hound* in London or the MFHA (Masters of Foxhounds Associa-

*Fig 3   The Brocklesby Hunt on arable land in Lincolnshire.
Hunting, shooting, farming and conservation all go hand-in-hand
here.*

tion), who are certain to be helpful (their telephone numbers are in the Useful Addresses on page 124), or consult *Baily's Hunting Directory*, published annually by J. A. Allen. Many local papers publish details of the meets through the season and a few will even give hunt reports, though gone are the days when papers like the *Daily Telegraph* do so.

Masters of Foxhounds Association

The governing body of the sport is the Masters of Foxhounds Association, who keep a register of all recognised packs of foxhounds and their boundaries, arbitrate if necessary on matters between hunts, and have an established set of rules for fox-hunting and considerable sanctions with which to enforce them.

The Secretary

From the Secretary will come details of the days on which the pack meets, and the cost of a subscription for a full season, or of a cap for a visitor. Subscriptions vary enormously, not only from hunt to hunt but even within a hunt. A rural hunt in west Wales without huge overheads costs a great deal less than a fashionable shires one, while a 'suburban' pack will come somewhere in between.

In many areas, farmers will hunt free of charge, or for kind rather than cash (i.e. they donate fallen stock to the kennels, or provide a quantity of hay or oats). In a remote farmers' pack it would not be practicable for farmers not to pay anything as that would leave almost no subscribers, and so each hunt sorts out its finances in the way best suited to it. The

9

Wigtownshire in south-west Scotland numbers just nineteen members, yet they are able to keep a pack of hounds and a professional huntsman, and show good sport.

Popular Days

Very often, it will be a Saturday that will cost more because of its popularity with those who cannot get away from work in the week, or else it will be the 'prime' days, for within most packs there are certain areas of its country which are considered better than others, and these will be hunted on a regular day of the week. For instance, in the four-day-a-week Quorn country, subscriptions for hunting on a Monday and Friday are a great deal more than on a Tuesday and Saturday.

In addition to the subscription, there will be field or 'wire fund' money to pay with many packs on each day out, which varies and is used specifically to mend fences or make good any damage. The subscription money goes towards hunt staff wages and the cost of kennelling, etc. The visitor's cap is inclusive, but generally one cannot expect more than three days per season with one hunt by this method.

Fig 4   The Ystrad Hunt passing a working coal mine in Wales.

Following on Foot

By far the best thing to do before delving straight into which sub to pay is to come out with the hunt first on foot. Try to visit with someone who knows what is happening or, failing that, see if the Secretary can point you in the direction of a knowledgeable car follower who is willing to help. In this way the dress can be noted and it will be seen, too, just how many different types of people and horses come out hunting. Most of them look smart (keeping up standards does not turn them into snobs) while there will always be one or two who look rough and ready. In Chapter 5 we will look at how to tell who is who and at the practical reasons behind the hunting apparel.

The Meet

The most usual time for the meet is 11 a.m. (although some meet at 10.45 a.m.) and it will usually be about ten or fifteen minutes later that hounds move off. (Note, hounds without 'the' in front of them is usual hunting language in this context — dogs never!)

The meet may be at a pub, a rural crossroads or at the home of a member who dispenses hospitality (usually port and/or sherry, or a hot red wine cup and possibly small hot sausage rolls, fruit cake or some other goody), and this is known as a lawn meet. Wherever the meet, the pack of hounds is usually taken to a prominent corner where they are patted by children and old hunt stalwarts, with the whipper-in preventing them from straying too far among the mingling horses and people.

Moving Off

The Master will decide when to move off and the huntsman will then give a short toot on the horn as a signal. Everyone else stands back to let them through, and another day's hunting begins.

With any luck, this first visit will be enough to encourage the newcomer to make his start. There will have probably been several very ordinary-looking horses among them and several positively sedate riders whom one could never imagine in a million years jumping huge fences.

But wasn't it exciting when the first 'music' (hounds may 'make music', 'speak', 'give tongue' or 'cry' but they *never* bark) was heard in the covert (do not pronounce the 't'), as hounds found a fox and began to give tongue, just a whimper or two at first, then a rousing, spine-tingling chorus as the whole pack joined in, crashing through the undergrowth? Then the sound the waiting field had been hoping to hear, the holloa from the whipper-in on point alone on the far side of the wood. He has waited until the fox is too far clear of the wood to change his mind and head back at the whip's yell. Instead, he lengthens his stride, lowers his mask and increases his pace.

Hounds hunt joyously through the wood and out into the open where their sound alters slightly, and, as they settle to their task, the huntsman blows 'Gone away'. This is the signal for the Field Master that he may bring the field on, and so their hunt begins.

There is no other feeling on earth quite like it, and although the story of a man's three favourite things in life being 'a good day's hunting, a day's hunting and a bad

11

Fig 5 *'Gone away' – and for the mounted followers the hunt begins.*

Fig 6 *For the love of it.*

day's hunting' may be apocryphal, nevertheless it is no exaggeration to say that this is exactly how the sport grips some people. They need not be the jumping people, either, for there is so much else to absorb. Even on a bad day, they are out in the marvellous British countryside, taking in the sights and sounds, thinking out different ways of beating the cold, enjoying the social chit-chat, sharing the comradeship of a faithful hunter, and above all – the most absorbing thing – watching hounds at work.

You can go hunting anywhere in Britain as a complete stranger and know that you will meet people of similar ilk and interest, enjoying fresh air and exercise, beautiful and varied surroundings and at the same time being part of a time-honoured and truly fascinating tradition.

2 Choosing your Hunter

One of the many pleasures of hunting is the rapport that you establish with your horse, who will become your friend and confidant over the seasons. But how do you go about finding him? It may be that in the first place you look you strike it lucky, or it may be after months or even years of searching.

The biggest mistake you can make when you are just starting to hunt is to go for something that is too good for you, something flashy. It is all too easy to have mishaps with a patent safety, let alone something that looks good but is in fact way out of your ability range. It is important also to consider things like your weight and the type of country you want him for.

Another common mistake, in my view, is that people will insist on a young horse, when an older one should be far safer for the novice rider. Often even ten is considered too old, and twelve positively geriatric, yet, with ponies in particular, they should have many good years of service left to offer at that age.

Teenagers, especially, want to look good. Parents want their young children to look good. But the young person of either category who plumps for the 'handsome is what handsome does' is going to get much further in the hunting field and, more to the point, stay in it much longer, probably for a lifetime. Nothing will put a child off hunting quicker than over-facing him with his mount.

How to Find your Hunter

The first horse or pony should have been hunting before, and somehow or other you must discover what you can about his reputation in the hunting field. A horse, or in particular a pony, can be as good as gold at home, meek and mild, but can be transformed into the devil personified at the sight and sound of hounds, pulling hard, running away and being generally out of the terrified rider's control.

The Local Paper

My son was almost twelve before restarting riding and coming out hunting for the first time and, as a consequence, many of his friends were far ahead of him both in ability and experience. Of the first two ponies I looked at, one was too small (my mistake) and the next appeared to be perfect – until I took him for a ride in the woods. There he tried to run away with me at the trot.

We were luckier with the third pony, an elderly pony of sixteen who was advertised in the local paper for a three-figure price. For seven years Nina had done no more than hack around the farm (and was adept at opening and shutting gates, useful in itself), with occasional days' hunting and competing in local hunter trials. No one can say she is the finest-bred hunter but she does the job of schoolmistress to perfection. She is no slug but easy to hold, and ordinary-sized

Fig 7 A perfect pair – mother and daughter on matching piebalds.

hunt jumps are well within her capabilities. Being bought from the local paper, it was easy enough to check up about her before committing myself. In no time at all, my son was hooked on hunting, and a very large part of the credit for that goes to the pony. She undoubtedly gave him the confidence that some of his more experienced friends were losing through being 'over-horsed'.

A local paper is a good way of finding a hunter, whether you want a horse or a pony. The chances are that if there is something really amiss in terms of temperament or soundness, the vendor is not going to want to risk his reputation in the area.

Horse and Hound

The choice in a local paper will not be as great as that to be found in the columns of *Horse and Hound*, but with the latter, in no time at all, you can find yourself travelling literally hundreds of miles in vain pursuit of your paragon.

We once sold a youngster to the then advertising manager of *Horse and Hound*. He returned a week after his first visit and said that of all the animals he had visited, ours was the only one that actually tallied with the description in the advertisement! People are inclined to advertise what they think you want rather than what they have actually got. Thus, a fine-boned

15

15.3hh. becomes a 16hh. middleweight, etc.; and once a horse is twelve or so, and its precise age becomes harder to determine, you may be sure a vendor will err on the younger side!

Word of Mouth

Without doubt, the best way of finding your ideal hunter is by word of mouth, but the fact that you are only just starting to hunt makes that very possibility harder for you – unless it is because you have good friends who hunt that prompts you to take it up. Whatever the case, if you are lucky enough to have a personal recommendation, then so much the better.

Dealers

The next best method may be to go through a dealer, preferably a local one – but there are dealers and dealers, of course. Find a reputable one, people will tell you, but how do you know which is which when you are starting out? Some will operate from run-down little back-street premises using every trick in the book while others will be the epitome of respectability, adhering to an agreed code of conduct.

As with most things in life, it is inclined to be the minority who spoil things for the majority. But shady dealers do exist. I felt fairly apprehensive when I went to a dealer for the first time. What clinched it for me was his assurance that should the horse prove unsuitable (regardless of having been passed by the vet), he would take it back. This proved unnecessary, and further purchases were made from him subsequently. Obviously it is in the dealer's own interests not to take advantage of you, and he will probably go to

considerable lengths to try to find the right horse to suit you, once he knows exactly what you are looking for.

The best thing, if possible, is to see if you may have a day's hunting on the horse. Trial facilities may not only be limited but also so well known to the horse himself that it cannot be a trial in the true sense. Some vendors will allow a horse out on a week's trial, a gesture which never ceases to amaze me when one considers the risks involved. Should this be offered to you, accept the manna while taking every precaution possible that you do not abuse it. In particular, check insurance and responsibilities in case anything should go wrong. If the vendor should offer you a day or half a day's hunting, when he will almost certainly be present, you should jump at the chance.

Livery Proprietors or Riding Schools

It may also be possible to find the right horse through either of the above, especially if you are planning to keep your horse at livery or even take riding lessons on him. Again, it will be in the proprietor's own interests to find a horse that suits your own needs.

Sales

Sales are not to be recommended for the beginner or one-horse owner. You can strike it lucky, but often the horses are there for a reason. Making sure you buy one warranted sound is no solution if in fact the reason the horse is there is because it is extremely nappy. You may pick up a bargain but such purchases are not to be recommended for the novice.

Specialized hunter sales are held at various venues, notably Leicester, and also Newbury, Melton Mowbray, Hereford, Taunton and such places. At Leicester, horses may be tried out in a paddock area with schooling fences before the sales begin, and warranted horses are vetted by the sale's vet on site before the purchase is completed, but I would still rate this type of purchase better left to the expert.

What to Look For

In general, it is better to buy while the hunting season is still in progress so that you can see what the horse is like then. A summer at grass could mask all sorts of faults: an 'iffy' leg may have had time to return to normal but could be something that may recur once hard work recommences in the autumn; or the horse may have fattened up, hiding the fact that during the season he looked like a hat-rack either because he is a 'poor doer' or a constant worrier.

You must make sure your prospective hunter has good bone, i.e. that he is not spindly beneath the knee, and that he is up to your weight. We are not talking about an hour's hack or a five-minute hunter trial, but four or five hours in the hunting field humping you about.

Temperament is very important. When you first start hunting, you do not want to be worrying about what new-fangled bit to try out this time to try to hold him in. Neither do you want a horse that is nappy, although when you start hunting you are nearly always going to be in among the crowd and most horses are amenable in those conditions. The odd buck from *joie de vivre* should be within

your capabilities on a non-thoroughbred (a thoroughbred's buck is bigger, quicker, and liable to include a drop of the shoulder while a non-thoroughbred type is liable to 'ask' you first for permission and be much easier to cope with), but do not consider a horse that shows any tendency to rear.

The horse world is full of various sayings, and most of them are bound up in the truth: 'no foot, no horse; no hock no hunter'. The foot is often the source of lameness. If a horse has feet which do not match, the chances are there is a problem with one, such as navicular disease. If he has thin soles or brittle hooves, he will be hard to keep sound, while the hock is especially important in a hunter as it has to propel hefty hindquarters through deep mud. 'Four white socks don't buy a horse' is meant to be a sign of temperament, but this one is not proven. White, however, is not only harder to keep clean but can be much more sensitive and therefore prone to mud fever.

Colour comes into it: for instance, 'There's no such thing as a bad roan'. My father once had a marvellously honest strawberry roan called Redskin, and Nina is a blue roan. There are not many roans, but this saying is probably based on experience. Similarly, you will be advised that chestnuts are hot, and that chestnut mares are hot and temperamental. By and large, chestnuts are hotter, but luckily there are exceptions to every rule. Two of the best mares I have ever ridden have been chestnuts with a lot of white about them. Certainly, if you find a good chestnut mare she will take some beating for she will be bold (but will probably know when to stop if over-faced) and wanting to please. Bay is the most common colour and is likely to be the one

Fig 8   A good type of hunter.

you go for, but there is nothing wrong with brown, grey (except in the cleaning), or liver chestnut. For some reason, blacks often seem to be a bit temperamental, and the only problem with buying a coloured horse (piebald, skewbald or even palomino) is that you are going to be very conspicuous, especially should anything go wrong, which you will not want as a newcomer.

You may well take a friend who is more of an expert than you are to see a horse, but remember a horse that suits you will not necessarily click with someone else. Always see a horse ridden by the vendor or his groom first. Another important point is to ensure that he is good in traffic. There is also a lot to be said for instinct and first impressions. It is

a good sign when you take an instant liking to a horse and it is even better when you still like the horse on second viewing!

I have purposely not gone into the finer points of what you should look for in terms of conformation and so forth. As long as you bear in mind the points that have been made and then, above all, submit your prospective purchase to a veterinary examination, you should not go too far wrong.

Vetting

Do not be tempted to forego this. It may cost quite a lot nowadays including VAT and travelling, but every penny has to be worth it. It is far better to spend for this purpose to avoid buying an unsuitable horse, than to shell out considerably more on one that is wrong.

The vet will check the heart, eyes, wind and action. He will not only spot lameness or conformation faults which will lead to lameness or pain (such as splints, wolf teeth, curbs, back-at-the-knee, etc.) but also vices (such as shying, rearing, box-walking, crib-biting or windsucking) and shivering (a complaint of the hind legs in which a horse cannot go backwards or balance himself if a hind foot is lifted) – not all of which you will have spotted for yourself!

Hiring

An option to consider before splashing out on buying a horse before hunting for the first time (unless you already own one, of course) is to hire. At first glance, the daily rate may seem high, especially when you have to pay a cap on top of that, but if you were to add up the cost of keeping a horse for the season, the price of hiring one for a few times pales into insignificance!

The best way to find a horse is to ask the hunt Secretary to tell you who hires out horses in the area and make further enquiries from there. One word: just because you are paying by the day for the horse and do not have to worry about what happens to him thereafter, that does not mean that you should not look after him as if he were your own. Occasionally one sees hirelings abused on the 'this is just a machine and I'm going to get my money's worth' basis but this is a deplorable attitude.

3 Keeping the Hunter

The main choices open to you are: (i) to keep the horse at home, (ii) to keep the horse at livery, or (iii) to keep the horse at do-it-yourself livery, but the outcome is likely to depend on your professional, financial and domestic circumstances. If you are in the fortunate position of having an open choice, there are various pros and cons to weigh up.

At Livery

If you keep the horse at livery, he will arrive for you spick and span (including being plaited), on time at the meet and will be taken away at the end of the day with no work involved for you whatsoever. You can simply flop in the bath and reminisce on your day. You will not be affected by labour shortages and you will have the freedom to go away at any time of the day or night without worrying about your charge as he will be kept fit and cared for.

Check the extras on the basic fee. These are likely to include blacksmith's and veterinary fees (including routine worming, teeth rasping, equine influenza and anti-tetanus vaccinations, etc.), and transport to and from the meet. Clipping is unlikely to be an extra charge, but for a horse which has to be bedded on shavings or paper instead of straw, you are likely to be charged the appropriate amount extra.

For those whose full-time work involves a lot of travelling, or who live out of the country (being based in London mid-week, for instance), livery will be the answer. Time, your own work and your own financial position all affect your choice, although personal inclination also comes into it. If you keep a horse at livery, you may go and ride out from time to time, especially in the autumn when you need to get your riding muscles into trim after the summer off, the same as your hunter. Livery proprietors are usually quite happy for you to do this as they can then deploy labour elsewhere, but it would be unreasonable to bring your horse back covered in mud and soaked with sweat. It would then take staff far longer to deal with him than had they taken him out on gentle road exercise themselves, to say nothing of it being unfair on an unfit horse.

Do-It-Yourself Livery

The DIY choice is most likely to apply if you do not own your own land or stable, and do not want, or cannot afford, full livery, and it is a good compromise.

The types of DIY available vary. You may simply pay a rent for the use of the stable and, presumably, water, and provide everything else yourself – food, hay, grooming and exercise – and you will then need to visit twice a day. Or it may include provision of hay and straw in the basic fee, or any combination of services including mucking out, etc. Obviously the price reflects the amount of extras included.

At Home

On the whole, by having a horse at livery you will miss the close connection and consequent affection that you gain when you keep your horse at home. I think this is one of the lovely parts of hunting, although I do not necessarily think so when I have mislaid some kit, or the telephone keeps going or the lorry refuses to start just when I am trying to get off in good time. And it can be very cold at the end of the day! However, there is usually a drive home rather than a hack, and as long as you keep a boot jack and spare footwear in the vehicle (which must have an efficient heater), as well as spare warm clothing, you should be warm and dry enough by the time you get home to see to your horse with good grace before attending to your own ablutionary and victual needs! If you employ a groom who will take the horse from you on your return, you probably have the best of both worlds.

Coming in from Grass

By August you will probably want to bring your hunter in from his summer grass, especially if you want to go cub-hunting. This will probably begin in September, depending on what sort of farming area you live in. Your hunter does not have to be super fit for cub-hunting. Indeed, it is a nice gentle way of getting your horse fit for hunting, but he does have to have done some work first.

That work must be walking only to begin with, followed by trotting. People are inclined to spell out a set number of weeks but the period for each depends a lot on your individual horse: whether he is a lightweight, the active sort who gets himself fit or the heavy, thick-winded type who needs longer. Whichever your horse, do not be tempted to rush. You want your horse's legs to be as hard as iron in order to withstand the rigours ahead in the hunting field.

Also, you do not want him getting saddle sores; remember his skin will be soft from lack of work. Neither do you want to go galloping him before his lungs are ready for it, or you could end up with respiratory problems. Patience is the answer on all counts. Take things gently at first and you will reap the dividends later.

If the early autumn is warm and you have the facilities, it is a good idea to start work while your horse is still at grass. Your horse is going to spend several months in his stable, so the longer he can stay out the better.

The best thing of all, where possible, is to continue to turn your horse out each day for a few hours right through the winter. In fact, when your horse is fully fit and hunting once or twice a week, he will need very little exercising in between if he is able to enjoy an hour or two at grass daily.

The Blacksmith

First of all, your horse will need to be shod, so make sure you have got the blacksmith arranged before you want to begin work. The insertion of road studs is generally a good idea. Let the blacksmith know that you would like him to visit on a regular basis throughout the winter and establish how much notice he requires before a visit. In some areas of the country there is a shortage of black-smiths, with fewer apprentices entering the trade in spite of the increase in riding horses for leisure, so try to make a firm arrangement in good time.

Occasionally, you may lose a shoe out hunting, and then of course you just hope your smith can fit you in at the earliest possible moment. Shoes are expensive to replace every three to five weeks and even more so when VAT is added, plus the cost of studs, and occasionally a travelling fee, too. However, do not be tempted to leave your next booking until the shoes are paper thin because they can cut legs like a knife out hunting. Equally, do not leave them with the nails pro-truding or you are then almost certain to lose at least one out hunting and will have to curtail the day's sport, for which you are paying a great deal more than one set of shoes! As a temporary measure, use a hammer to knock over any protruding nails.

Apart from the straightforward shoe-ing, your blacksmith can also carry out remedial work on the foot when required and will advise you about their care, especially where the horn is brittle or the sole thin. It is worth bearing in mind also that lameness can often emanate from the foot, and it is much cheaper to call out the blacksmith in the first instance than a vet. He may find a bruised sole, a corn (as painful in horses as they are in humans), or a tiny puncture wound where some-thing sharp has pierced the foot or a piece of grit has lodged. If the wall of the foot is warmer on the lame side than on the sound side, the likelihood is that the problem is in the foot, but also sometimes

swelling of the leg right up to the knee can be caused by rising poison in the foot.

Annual Inoculations

Equine Influenza

The best time to give your horse his annual vaccination booster is as soon as he comes in from his summer at grass. If you leave it until he is in fast work, that work will have to be halted for a few days as he must not be allowed to get in a sweat after this inoculation. Also, it can give some horses mild flu symptoms for a short period.

There is much controversy about flu jabs. Why give them when the horse can still fall foul of another variety, or to a virus with similar symptoms? It seems that as soon as one variety can be inocu-lated against, another emerges. Never-theless, it does offer valuable protection and should not be overlooked. Further-more, there is nothing more selfish than to come out hunting with a coughing horse – it spreads like wildfire.

Your vet will give you a vaccination certificate, filling in the details of the vaccination and, in many cases, he will telephone you the following year to remind you that the booster is due. When vaccinating against flu for the first time, there will be two injections, the second coming within twenty-one to ninety-two days of the first.

Anti-Tetanus

Equally important is the anti-tetanus injection; some areas have a high risk of infection. If you are not sure whether your horse has been innoculated against it and he sustains a cut, you must have him given a temporary (thirty-day) jab immediately. Tetanus is a terrible, frightening and usually incurable, disease.

It is worth noting here that humans, also, should keep their tetanus injections up to date. I remember a doctor once being amazed that I was nervous of having a jab yet unafraid of falling off! He pointed out that horse people were inclined to be particular about injecting their horses but neglectful about themselves, and tetanus is just as lethal for humans! In many cases, your horse will have a combined flu and tetanus jab, and this is the best thing to do.

Teeth Rasping

It is wise to have this annual dental check done by your vet at the same time as the vaccination. Horses' molar teeth get very sharp and need filing down, similar to human finger nails. A metal gadget is used to keep the mouth open, much like a jack on a car, and with the mouth thus open, the vet uses a long-handled rasp. It does not hurt the horse. The vet will also notice if there are any other dental problems, such as wolf teeth, which may need removing.

Worming

How many times do people have to be told to worm their horses regularly? Vets must despair when dealing with the aftermath of unwormed or insufficiently wormed horses, and in some cases the horse may die. If you have only a small paddock, you must remove the piles of droppings, no matter how tedious and, if possible, rotate your grazing (divide your one paddock to make two) in order to help prevent the pasture becoming 'horse sick'.

The most important time of a horse's life for worm control is as a youngster, so with your bought-in hunter you can only hope this was carried out. Otherwise, there may come a day when your horse suffers colic and, after heart-breaking pain and veterinary attention, some hours later he dies. It may then be found that he had an aneurism (a blood-filled sac protruding from an artery) that had blocked his intestine wall so that nothing could pass through, and death was therefore inevitable.

Your horse must be well wormed when he comes in from grass, and again two weeks later to get rid of the residual worms which had only been eggs during the first worming. He should then be wormed again at six-weekly intervals throughout the winter even though he is stable kept, and especially if he spends some periods out at grass.

Apart from the risk of death, a wormy horse may cough, become anaemic, stary-coated, ribby (no matter how well he is eating), and subsequent loss of performance is inevitable.

Feeding

Like most things with horses, feeding is largely a matter of common sense. I shall not give hard and fast rules for the amount to be fed, for this will differ even between horses of similar type who are doing the same amount of work because they are all individuals. There are, however, certain rules which must be adhered to:

(a) Feed little and often (the horse's stomach is small and by nature he is a grazer, not used to wolfing down large amounts in one sitting).

(b) Feed at regular times, at least within an hour either side of your normal time. If you get home late from work, you may have a horse so ravenous that he will gulp his feed down and promptly get colic. Try to make sure at the start of the season that you have a friend or neighbour you can call on at a moment's notice if you find yourself unavoidably delayed.

(c) Ensure that you make the transition from grass keep to hard concentrates gradually. This is where it helps if you start riding your horse from grass, or if he spends at least part of the day out at grass.

(d) Do not feed the current season's hay for the first few months. This is one of the most frequent causes of colic in the autumn.

(e) Do not feed the horse when he is hot or tired. Give a little warm mash after hunting, then his main feed later on. Likewise, if you do not have automatic water, water him before feeding rather than after. I prefer to keep water present at all times.

(f) Do not work your horse for an hour after feeding, just as you should not swim after a meal.

(g) Always feed best-quality food. If you cannot afford the fodder, you cannot afford a horse. There are certain things you can cut corners on in horse-keeping, but feeding is not one of them.

(h) Feed according to the work being done: lots of oats with lots of hunting, but cut right back when sidelined. Azoturia (see page 109) is a common result of a horse having had a day off without a reduction in his hard food.

(i) Do not let food go off or stale. Keep it fresh in airtight (and mouseproof) containers and feed it in clean containers.

There are all sorts of prepared foodstuffs and extras on the market, but you may do little better than to feed whole oats bought off a local farm and delivered in, along with soaked sugar-beet and molasses. You can add ordinary household salt, especially after your horse has been sweating, and cod liver oil.

If you want your horse to have less oats or you want to fatten him, boil some whole barley also bought from your tame farmer. This makes a nice hot feed. Oats, barley and sugar-beet pulp are all sources of protein and carbohydrates, as are flaked maize, hay, grass and horse nuts or mix. Fat is obtained from linseed, soya bean meal, milk pellets, horse nuts, grass meal, barley and maize. The essential minerals such as calcium and potassium are found in grass and grains. Sufficient vitamins should also be present in the fodder, and feeding carrots will give extra vitamins, so the need to give mineral additives should be comparatively rare.

At the start of the season, weigh your bowlful of oats so that you know exactly what you are feeding. Animals in light work need approximately seventy per cent hay to hard food, fifty to sixty per cent in medium work and only twenty to thirty per cent when in hard work. However, do not be afraid to use proprietary foodstuffs. A great deal of research goes into their make-up to ensure a balanced and nutritional diet, and, because of the requirements of the Rules of Racing, much care to ensure that none of it is contaminated in any way. It may cost you more than buying direct from a farmer, but you can rest assured about its quality and its ease of feeding.

Water

Your horse will drink between six and twelve gallons of water a day, depending on his size, on the weather, and whether he has dry or damp food, so a plentiful supply is essential. He will drink less at grass as this has a high moisture content.

Over half your horse's body-weight will be made up of water. Water maintains his body fluids, helps with his digestion and maintains his body temperature. The only times he should not have water available are when he comes home from hunting (he may have a little, but it should have some hot water added to it to take the chill off), immediately after feeding (unless he has had all he needs before feeding), and for three or four hours before fast work.

He may well be dehydrated after hunting, and then the little and often rule applies. If you allow him to gulp down a bucketful he may well get colic. I have one hunter who likes to drink a bit while out hunting, and this I allow him to do, again in very small doses. No more than three sips or one gulp is a sensible rule.

Some people do not like automatic water systems on the grounds that they do not know how much the horse is drinking. It is comparatively rare, however, that you actually need to know this, but if you do, it is easy enough to cover the automatic supply bowl and provide a bucket. You can also adopt this method

after hunting, in order to give your horse some warmer water. On the other hand, he can drink only a fairly small amount at a time from the automatic drinker, and then has to wait for it to fill up again. The biggest advantage of the automatic water is that there is a permanent supply. Your horse cannot knock the bucket over or, if you are late home from work, he does not have to wait.

You may occasionally need to clean out the automatic drinker, if some fodder or straw gets in it. Have it placed about half-way up the wall, so that it is within comfortable reach for him, and not so low that straw or droppings get into it.

Grooming

Ideally, your horse should be strapped (groomed) daily, and if you have a groom or keep the horse at livery, he most certainly will be. However, if you are in full-time work, you may sometimes only be able to pay lip-service to grooming. I know that a good strapping helps muscle up and tone your horse and improve his coat, but adequate work should also achieve the former, and plentiful good-quality food the latter. You can get away with putting a brush over him before exercise, and you must always pick out his feet to prevent him getting thrush (a very smelly complaint caused by standing on muck), and to remove any stones or grit picked up when he was outside.

Although it will look nice to have a silken, beautifully brushed mane and tail, this is not actually going to improve your horse's health or performance, and can be dispensed with except on a hunting morning. If he sweats up on exercise, this

25

must be brushed off with a soft body brush when it is dry, and the same applies to mud. The trick, once your horse is hunting fit and only needs 'ticking over' in between, is to keep him both dry and clean on exercise!

It is all too easy for a horse to get mud fever in the hunting season, or cracked heels (the equivalent of badly chapped hands in a human). They can crack wide open, bleed and be exceedingly sore. Pale-skinned or white-legged horses are especially susceptible. A very good prevention tip is to spread plenty of petroleum jelly in his heels before hunting. Some land areas are more prone to mud fever than others, but the best answer is not to take any risks.

You must get all the mud off his heels, fetlocks, belly, elbows and between his hind legs after hunting, and if you use water for this, you must dry them as well. Occasionally you will be able to wash off your horse on the way home in a brook or pond (make sure it is known to have a safe bottom before you wade in).

Quite often if we finish at a farm some way from home, I am able to borrow a hose-pipe while waiting for transport to arrive (even though I have no groom or driver, people all help each other at the end of the day; often I will lead someone's horse off mine while they are given a lift to the horse-boxes). There are two schools of thought on the use of a hose-pipe, but all I can say is that it is jolly useful to have one handy. If I am going to hose a horse, I prefer to do it while he is still warm and wet. If there is no chance before arriving home and he has then dried off, I am loath to get him wet and cold again.

My palomino does not like to be unduly disturbed at the end of a long, hard day, and I will do little more than get the worst off him with a brush. Some people will throw their hands up in horror but, in my experience, if I fiddle about with him for long, he breaks out in a sweat, goes off his food, and ends up much more uncomfortable than if he had been left in peace, no matter how much mud has been left on him. I always check round last thing and then, finding all well, leave him until the morning.

Clipping

Your hunter will need to be clipped, to avoid excess sweating and to make him easier to clean off and dry off after hunting. He will probably need clipping every three weeks from October to at least January. Later clips can interfere with the growth of his summer coat. If you have only one horse and you work full time, it will probably be a good idea to have your horse clipped for you, especially if he is ticklish or generally difficult to do. New clippers vary in price so, with probably at least four clips needed per season, it is going to be worth while buying your own if you can then find the time or help when needed.

There are several different types of clip, and the choice will be up to you and your circumstances. For a *full clip*, the whole coat is removed. Occasionally this is done on a hunter for the first clip of the season, but I would not recommend it for anything but a hairy-coated horse.

A thoroughbred-type needs the extra protection under the saddle and on the legs that a *hunter clip* gives, and this is the most usual clip for hunting, hence its name. You may prefer, however, to give a *blanket clip*, which keeps the coat on in the shape of a blanket. This is useful if you are able to turn him out by day in the winter (but he must also wear a New Zealand rug), if he particularly feels the cold, or if you do not anticipate a tremendous amount of hard work. The same applies more so to a *trace clip*, which also keeps in half the neck and the head. I have sometimes kept the head in anyway for horses that feel the cold.

A *belly clip* just takes out the lower half of the belly, between the front legs and perhaps a thin line up the neck. This is ideal for a pony to stay warm enough when kept out, whose owner wants to be able to hunt as soon as he gets home from boarding school without the pony sweating up excessively.

It is common practice to trim the whiskers around the horse's muzzle and eyes, and probably his heels. It is also usual to trim about an inch of mane on the poll where the headpiece of the bridle goes.

Mane and Tail

The horse's mane should be pulled, never cut, at the beginning of the season to make it neat and encourage it to lay over on one side (preferably to the right). It is best to pull it after exercise when the horse is warm, as the hair comes away more easily and less painfully. If your horse gets sore, only do a little at a time.

Most hunters have their tails pulled, too. An alternative is to plait the tail for hunting, and many people will also tie up the tail once the ground gets wet and muddy. This not only keeps it cleaner but prevents the horse having to carry a heavy, bedraggled wad of tail behind him. If your horse has a nice, neat tail, there is no need to do anything to it other than have it well brushed out before hunting.

4 Clothes and Tack

Clothes

In spite of the bias of certain citizens hell-bent on believing that hunting people are toffee-nosed, not least because of the clothes they wear, it will be seen that nearly all the apparel has a practical reason for being as it is. For instance, the hunting tie not only protects the neck but also acts as an instant bandage when needed in an emergency. The red coat, worn only by servants, Masters and some subscribers (generally those who have the hunt button – *see* page 57), can be picked out in the distance on a grey winter's day, and since the people wearing them are those who should be roughly in the right place at the right time, this is very useful to those who also want to be there!

However, I say nearly everything has a practical use, because a strong case can be made to say that the top hat is now obsolete and will eventually die out completely (more of that later). Indeed, let us begin at the top, and work downwards.

Headwear

What a ticklish subject this has become and yet it should not be so. The headwear available is the hunting cap, the top hat, the bowler hat, the skull cap and the riding hat with harness, and even, out cub-hunting, the tweed cloth cap! Dyed-in-the-wool traditionalists say they will never wear a hat with a harness.

The day will come when everyone does, of this I am convinced, even if it takes a law to enforce it. People claimed the seat-belt law would be unenforceable, especially as many people said they would never wear them. Yet look what a success this law has been and, more importantly, look how many lives have been saved.

Hunting should set its example from the top, as racing has done, insisting that crash caps are not only worn when racing but by stable staff at all times when mounted. Sadly, it does not do so. Yet there have been a number of deaths and terrible head injuries which would have been much lessened had the safer head-gear been worn.

The road, as I explain in Chapter 8, is lethal. If you hit the road from a height of, say, four feet at a trotting speed of six to eight miles per hour and your hat falls off before you hit the ground head-first, desperate injury to yourself, worry and shock for those around you and work for hospital staff can be the only result.

The wearing of a modern safety hat with harness fastened is said to reduce the risk of head injury from sixty per cent to fifteen per cent, a statistic that speaks for itself, but still there are those who believe it will never happen to them. In honesty, their policy is a selfish one, for it is not 'their own business and nobody else's' as many declare. Those left to care for them come into it too.

Traditions evolve over the years. There never were hard and fast rules over dress, but certain things gradually be-

Fig 9   Chin-straps are worn increasingly out hunting as a safety measure.

came established practice. There has to be room for change, as times change.

In the earliest years, riding caps were worn, but in the nineteenth century the top hat and red coat became fashionable, while the farmer retained the cap and black coat. Today people say they cannot differentiate between hunt servants and Masters and everyone else if they all wear caps, but it is not that difficult if you take the trouble. Other tell-tale signs come with the hunt coats; hunt servants have five buttons, Masters four, farmers and subscribers three.

In the early 1980s, as some responsible people began wearing caps instead of top hats, grey caps were brought in for subscribers to mark the difference. Traditionally, farmers and Masters keep the ribbons on at the back of their cap, subscribers cut them off or sew them up inside the cap.

Handmade hunting caps of traditional style will come off in certain circumstances, no matter what the wearer says to the contrary. Some people have these hats fitting so tightly to the head in order to avoid losing them that they must surely go home every time with a headache.

The British Standards Institute has a hunting cap with harness, BS 6473, and a crash cap, BS 4472, which conform to the best safety standards so far produced and

Fig 10 The top-hat is still worn, but the hunting cap with harness is being increasingly recognized as safer.

look smart in the hunting field. The skull cap should be worn with a velvet cover (the silk cover is for eventing). These caps will seem perfectly smart once they are accepted by all, as they are in racing and, of course, polo. The Pony Club took a stand in 1986 when it made the wearing of the crash cap BS 4472 compulsory for all Pony Club members out hunting (and at all Pony Club ridden functions).

A few ladies and some grooms or men still wear bowler hats out cub-hunting, while just a few men still wear a cloth cap.

The only other thing to remember about the head is for ladies to wear a hairnet (unless their hair is very short), and remember to keep a few spare ones in your pocket. There will be certain bushes within your hunt which produce a bumper crop of lost hairnets each year! Long hair should be tied back in a pony tail, preferably with a ribbon to match your coat. Even men with very long hair will wear a pony tail!

The wearing of ear-rings is frowned upon. As usual, there is a practical reason as well as social, for an ear-ring caught in a thorn bush could cause a very nasty torn ear.

Hunting Stock or Tie

Next we come to the neck. Children should wear a tie, adults should wear a tie out cub-hunting or a coloured stock (hunting tie), and at all other times a white or cream silk or cotton stock. It is fashionable nowadays to refer to a stock as a hunting tie (it being pointed out that stock are animals), but how many words are there in the English language with double or even treble meanings? Stock, after all, could also go with shares. (It is the same with scarlet coats. No longer are we supposed to call them pink – Pink was a tailor, we keep being told – and yet when I grew up one definitely did not refer to a red coat, which has now become the in term.)

A tie or stock pin should preferably be a plain gold bar. Servants wear theirs vertically and followers should wear theirs horizontally (which means it is less likely to pierce the neck or scratch the face in the event of a fall).

Wear the stock as comfortably tight as you can, and make sure it is secured both

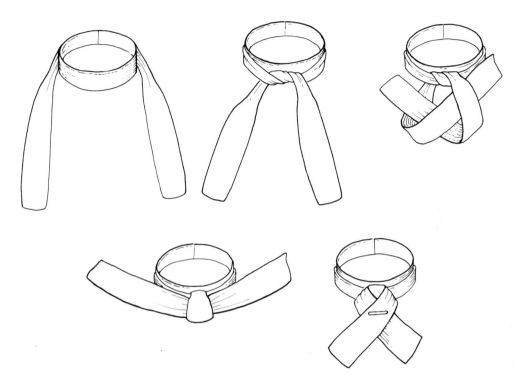

Fig 11   How to tie a hunting stock.

back and front. Gaps between stock and shirt are not only unsightly but also cause cold draughts. Worn with a hunting shirt, there should be button or stud holes for this purpose.

First, before putting it on, thread the long end through the gap left at the top of the short end until it is in a circle big enough to put your head through. Then slip it over your head, and align it as you tighten it so that front and back button holes match those on your shirt; then secure those. Now make a knot, keeping the material smooth and neat; then, in turn, lift each end to cross each other and, on the smooth piece between them, secure your pin, making sure it catches

the knot as well as the ends to keep them neatly in place. Finally, secure the tails with safety pins. This will prevent the ends from flapping out, and also means you have some safety pins in case of emergency. A stock may be shaped but may also be tied using long white rectangular material. The stock should be white cotton for men and white cotton or cream silk for women. Coloured or spotted ones may be worn with rat-catcher (*see* page 80).

Hunting Shirt and Waistcoat

It is advisable to buy a purpose-made hunting shirt, which will be collarless and

31

have the appropriate holes for fixing the stock. Try to get one with the arms and back long enough to help keep you warm. Most shirts are made of cotton, though some are of thick brushed cotton for extra warmth. It is advisable to have a thinner one for warmer weather and a really thick one for cold days. If you feel the cold, a vest is an enormous help, too. For cub-hunting, an ordinary check shirt is sufficient. This can also be worn when wearing ratcatcher for any reason during the season, such as when on gate-shutting duty.

A quilted waistcoat may be worn, but a woollen hunting waistcoat of either yellow or check is much nicer. I have inherited a suede leather one which is a beauty and remarkably warm. A V-neck jumper, with or without sleeves, may also be worn.

Hunting Jacket

Here again, you may spend a fortune on a made-to-measure article, or you may pick one up second-hand. If the latter, or off-the-peg, try to ensure it is a good fit (allowing room for a jumper to be worn underneath). It will make all the difference to looking smart. You will want one with three buttons down the front. We will assume that, as a starter to hunting, you are not wearing a scarlet coat. You are also more likely to wear a skirted coat with rounded edges than a swallow-tailed one. The latter looks very dashing on a slim young blade who has hunted all his life, but you are unlikely to be wanting to draw attention to yourself!

A lady should wear a midnight blue or black coat. For some infuriating reason, makers are inclined to make ladies' coats of a lighter weight than men's and, while they look smart, the cold can be unbearable. So again, try and get as warm a one as you can and, whatever you do, do not get a lightweight showing jacket!

When it comes to cleaning jackets, remember these are not for the washing machine or hot water as they will shrink. It is a tedious question of letting them dry and then cleaning off the mud with a stiff brush (a dandy brush is excellent for this, as long as you keep it in the house and do not use it on a horse). Sometimes I scrape chunks of mud off with the back of a knife before brushing.

A really muddy jacket can be hosed down, or scrubbed with rain water; the excess water must be allowed to drip off before the coat is put near any heat. By this method it will take some days to dry, so a second coat will also be needed if hunting again soon. Also, sometimes when the jacket has dried, you will find you have not cleaned it as well as you thought you had when it was wet; you may find water rings remaining, so you will still need a stiff brush.

Of course, there is another marvellous method of cleaning the coat – take it to the dry cleaners! It costs more money, of course, and most dry cleaners will insist on you getting the worst of the mud off first, but it will come back to you looking very smart.

Underclothes

Warm underclothes are a must, including (when it is really cold) longjohns and thermal vests. Men may also wear ladies' tights, especially if they are wearing nylon breeches. Silk is supposed to be as warm as anything and not so bulky to wear; both vests and socks can be obtained in silk. I would also advise thick socks, so make sure your boots are big enough to accommodate them.

Breeches

If you possibly can, do buy woollen breeches. Not only do they look really smart, but they are so much warmer. However, more and more people today wear stretch nylon breeches, and they are marvellous for cleaning as you simply pop them in the washing machine (but do up the velcro fastenings first, or the velcro will scuff patches of the breeches).

With a black coat you will probably wear fawn or beige breeches, although white is permissible, with plain boots. Ladies do not wear white breeches, but they may wear cream, beige or fawn. With nylon breeches you are unlikely to have knee buttons, which the woollen or cord ones will have. You will need a button hook for doing the latter ones.

Again, there is a world of difference in price between made-to-measure Melton cloth breeches by a London tailor and off-the-peg stretch ones. If you go for stretch, try to get the fairly robust sort. It is often possible to buy second-hand ones, quite often at a saddlers, or there are one or two shops which specialize in second-hand hunting clothes, such as the Uppingham Dress Agency in Leicestershire and Calcutt and Son in Sutton Scotney, Hampshire.

Boots

Once again, it is a case of 'you pays your money and you takes your choice'. If you can afford them, made-to-measure leather hunting boots are quite simply the best. When you go for measuring, however, make sure you wear your thickest pair of hunting socks. If you do not have room to wiggle your toes, cold feet will follow, no matter how expensive your boots.

Today, as with nylon breeches, so many people wear rubber boots, and great advances have been made in their design so that it is often quite difficult to tell them apart from leather. They are extremely convenient, needing only a wipe over to clean them, unlike the washing, drying, polishing and buffing of leather boots. But not only are they colder, they also offer less protection than a leather boot. This is an important advantage as it is only too easy to catch one's leg on a gatepost or tree or, worse still, to be kicked by another horse.

Spurs

Spurs are worn out hunting, but generally only to complete the outfit and so are small and blunt. Make sure you do not wear them upside down. The neck should face downwards, and the longer end of the spur should be on the outside of the boot. They should not be worn too low, but should rest where the foot of the boot meets the leg of the boot.

Whip

You should carry a hunting whip, also known colloquially as a crop, complete with thong and lash. The handle end is shaped in a hook which is useful for pulling a gate towards you or pushing it away. You may like to practise cracking your whip at home, but this is not something you will be doing in the hunting field. The most you will use the thong for is to lower it to the ground as hounds pass, to keep them away from your horse (but not to hit them).

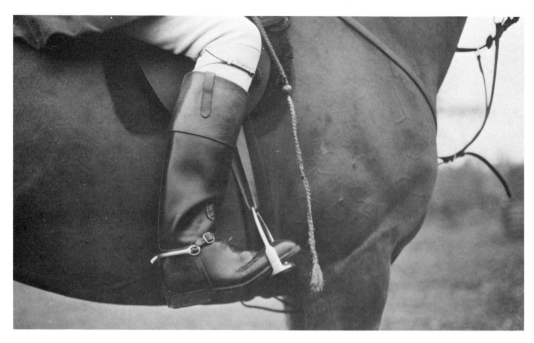

Fig 12   *A correctly fitted spur. This rider has a black boot with mahogany top, and a white garter strap with a buckle on the knee.*

Fig 13   *The thong of the hunting whip.*

Fig 14   Col. Neil Foster, a noted former Master and rider to hounds, showing the correct way to hold a hunting whip. His horse is wearing a double bridle and Grakle noseband.

You will hold your hunting whip and thong at the handle end, the remainder of the stick part lying across the withers and the thong hanging down at your horse's side. If the thong is rather long, you may also hold a circle of it.

If you find this too bulky, or for some reason believe you will want a sharper whip on your horse, many people hunt with a cutting whip. Try to stick to a leather-covered rather than a brightly-coloured one. The main disadvantage is at gates or when hounds are about, but otherwise you may find it more comfort-able. This should never be carried across the withers or pointing upwards (as is sometimes seen by show-jumpers), but should drop neatly downwards.

Gloves

Do not forget gloves; not only for neatness, they are also necessary. No matter how warm the morning, it may be very cold by late afternoon. Also, if your horse sweats or if it is raining, gloves will help you hold the reins.

Traditionally, yellow or white string

Fig 15   A correct turn-out.

gloves are worn, but again there are innovations, and today many people are wearing the cheaper pimpley gloves, mostly available in black, brown or fawn. They have pimples made of PVC on the palms for extra grip and are made of slightly elasticated knitted nylon which is quite warm; they also machine-wash well.

Try to get those with as long a wrist as possible, as any gaps of flesh attract cold. You will find you can afford several pairs, so get the same colour in order to match up lost ones. I once found I had four left hands, but I simply put one on the wrong hand, and I do not think many people noticed that I had the pimples pointing upwards. If you buy one bigger pair, you can wear thin liner gloves underneath on cold days.

Alternatively, there are really warm all-woollen gloves on the market (be careful how you wash them), and more expensive but very smart leather and string gloves.

Tack

Keep a separate, best set of tack for hunting and do not be tempted to use it for exercising. You will probably exercise in a plain snaffle, but may very well need something offering greater control in the hunting field. Even the quietest horse at home will be much more alert out hunting, while ponies can turn into devils personified, to the great terror of the unfortunate children riding them.

The reason for keeping a separate set is that it will be under much more strain out hunting and does not want the added burden of daily wear and tear on it. Keep it well cleaned and oiled (at all times of the year). Some people, once they need to have tack mended, immediately relegate it to exercising tack.

The Bridle

This must be made of English leather (not Indian leather or nylon, which may be used for exercising), and should have pimpled rubber-covered reins for good grip, unless they are of the plaited leather variety. Make sure the reins are long enough for you to slip them through your hands (referred to on page 81), but not so long that you run the risk of getting the end hooked up in your foot.

Nosebands

Use a neat noseband and browband (not coloured or fancy) and make sure it all fits nicely. It should be buckled so that you can fit two fingers in the gap between the nose and the band. For extra control, very often a drop or Grakle noseband is sufficient and is a very useful aid. Any of these will stop the horse opening his mouth to avoid the bit, and stop it yawning. Pressure is also placed on the bridge of the nose to stop him pulling.

A *drop* noseband, as the name implies, is fitted below the bit instead of above it, and again prevents the horse from opening his mouth or crossing or locking his jaw to evade the bit. Many people today use a *flash* noseband, which is similar to the *Grakle* but has the advantage that the flash part is detachable and so may at other times be used as a normal cavesson noseband.

For a really hard puller, the most effective noseband I have found is the *Kineton*. This is a device with semi-circles of metal which are hooked around the bit,

Fig 16 *A standing martingale and flash noseband. The rider is wearing a waterproof coat instead of a hunting jacket.*

Fig 17   A head study of a hunter wearing a snaffle bit and Grakle noseband. Note the rein stoppers to prevent the martingale rings getting caught in the rein buckles by the bit.

Fig 18   A Kineton noseband.

bringing pressure on the nose rather than on the bars of the mouth.

Bits

The Snaffle If a snaffle is sufficient for your horse out hunting, then stick to it. Do not change for change's sake as some horses hate being messed about. My father often used to have a twisted snaffle in his strong pulling cobs but I do not think these are seen so often nowadays.

The Double Bridle Traditionally, horses are hunted in a double bridle, but these are not seen very often nowadays (although there are plenty in the shires)

39

Fig 19 *A smart Pony Club turn-out. The pony is wearing a plain snaffle.*

and, as a newcomer to hunting, you are unlikely to be advised to use one. If you are, make sure your adviser also instructs you in its use.

A double bridle has two bits: the bridoon bit, which is generally smaller than a snaffle, and a curb or pelham bit. The curb, in conjunction with a curb chain, is the stronger, and the curb reins (below the bridoon reins) are used when extra braking power or control is needed. Otherwise they are held slightly slacker than the bridoon or snaffle rein and they are also narrower.

The snaffle rein is held through the second and third finger, and the curb rein through the third and fourth finger. The curb chain is attached to the bit by a hook and it must be fitted so that it rests in the groove of the jaw just above the lower lip (adjust it by hooking it on the appropriate link of the chain). It works through

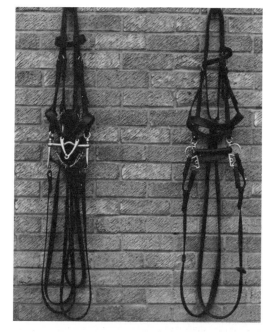

Fig 20 *A double bridle (left), and a straight-bar vulcanite Pelham.*

leverage. As the curb rein is used, so it tightens the chain against the jaw. The horse soon learns that by pulling less hard, the pressure against him will be reduced.

The Gag   The gag bit is ideal for the light-handed, but will be too severe for the rider with heavy hands. Once a horse learns he is going to be jabbed in the mouth over a fence, he will start refusing. To control the horse on the flat, the gag wants to be used by give and take from the rider's hands. The gag bit is attached to a rounded leather cheekpiece which passes through holes in the bit ring or through rollers or pulleys. The gag prevents a horse getting his head too low and thus restricts his ability to pull too hard.

The Pelham and Kimblewick   The Pelham combines in one bit the uses simi-lar to that of a double bridle, using a curb chain. It may have two reins or, by a connector on both rings, a single rein may be used which is easier for the less experienced rider. The bit may be jointed but is often a straight bar. Instead of metal, the bit is sometimes made of vulcanite or rubber, so that although it gives more control than a snaffle, it is nevertheless quite gentle on the mouth itself.

The Kimblewick is a type of Pelham with a port in its bar.

Saddles

The two most important points about the saddle are: (i) that it properly fits your horse and (ii) that you are comfortable in it. After that it does not matter too much, but you are nevertheless more likely to be comfortable in a conventional saddle.

The old-fashioned hunting saddle was very flat, both at the knees and in the seat. Today the trend is for a deeper seat with high cantle and knee rolls. The chief advantage here is one of comfort. A disadvantage, however, is that it keeps you too well in the saddle for, in the event of your horse falling, you will be better off thrown clear than pinned underneath. Knee rolls, too, are of no use if you like to ride fairly short as they get in the way and hurt.

One point to bear in mind about the fitting of the saddle is that while it may fit nicely on your well-rounded hunter in the autumn, by Christmas he may be leaner. You may need to have extra stuffing put in by your saddler, or perhaps use a thicker numnah – but do not use a numnah to disguise a poorly fitting saddle. It is most important that the saddle does not press down on the

Fig 21   A correctly fitted vulcanite Pelham.

withers, and that it should fit snugly, not at angles which will cause sores, with a clear channel along the spine.

Leathers, Irons and Girths Rule number one: all of the above must be unbreakable! The leathers should be made of cowhide, rawhide or buffalo hide and they may stretch. It is therefore a good idea to alternate the side of the saddle they are on, otherwise the left-hand side will stretch more through mounting.

You should buy stainless steel stirrup irons rather than nickel, and the width should be a little wider than your boot. If the irons are too wide, your foot may slip out too easily, and if too narrow, your foot could become dangerously wedged in the event of a fall. It is a good idea to place rubber grips in the foot of the stirrup iron. These give you extra grip and, to a certain extent, prevent the cold reaching your feet.

Young or novice children should have Peacock safety irons. These have the outside bar replaced by a stout rubber ring which, should the child be in danger of being dragged in a fall, will unfasten.

It is best to use a leather girth (but keep it well cleaned and oiled), and it is wise to buy the best you can afford. This should be either the three-fold variety (as the name implies, one piece of leather folded into three, which makes a smooth, comfortable and strong girth); the *Atherstone* girth, which is shaped at the elbows to avoid galling; or the *Balding* girth in which the leather is plaited, again leaving more room at the elbows.

Girths made of *lampwick* are very popular; they are soft, comparatively cheap and easy to clean. You can put them in a washing machine, preferably inside something like a pillow case to prevent the buckles damaging the machine. Other girths include *string nylon*, *webbing* (mostly used for racing and always worn in pairs) or *elastic*. Almost any girth can have a few inches of stout elastic added by the buckles for a bit of breathing space.

Martingales   Most people like a martingale of some type out hunting, not least because it provides a neck strap, and it is much better to hold that than hang on to the horse's mouth when your balance is awry. However, if you do not need a martingale, there is nothing wrong with fitting a neck strap only.

A *running martingale* splits into two at the chest, the two ends being attached by a ring to each rein. It offers extra control on a puller by providing further pressure on the reins and, through them, the mouth.

A *standing martingale* continues in one piece and is attached to the noseband. It will prevent the horse throwing his head too high.

A *breastplate* or *breastgirth* should be used in very steep country such as on Exmoor, or with the Clifton to prevent the saddle slipping.

Numnahs, Bandages and Boots

Strictly speaking, there is no need to use a numnah if the saddle fits correctly. However, they are increasingly used now, both for looks (not a bright colour out hunting, but maybe sheepskin) and for keeping the underneath of the saddle clean. The numnah can then simply be put in the washing machine.

I would never use bandages when out hunting. They can come untied and trail

Fig 22   *Three cheerful hunting farmers, well turned out for the day. Without the goodwill and co-operation of farmers and landowners, many of whom do not hunt themselves, hunting would not be able to survive.*

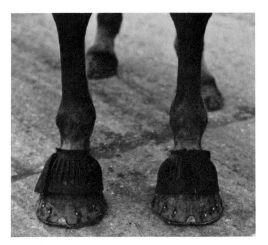

Fig 23   Correctly fitting over-reach boots.

loosely or, worse, as the horse warms up and his limbs swell a bit, they can become so tight and restrictive that permanent tendon damage can result.

Boots, such as brushing boots, are more a matter of choice and circumstance. They offer protection but, with mud or grit slipping inside and rubbing for several hours, can cause nasty sores. Generally, I go without. Over-reach boots, in theory, are excellent, especially in heavy ground or with a horse prone to clipping his front heels with his back feet. In reality, however, it is often in deep ground that the boot turns inside out, so becoming useless just when it is needed.

5 Who's Who

The Secretary

We have looked briefly at the role of the Secretary who, in addition to taking the caps and arranging subscriptions, acts as an important liaison between Master, hunt staff, farmers, subscribers and the committee.

Sometimes there will be joint Secretaries, especially where two packs have amalgamated. Occasionally he will wear an arm band to denote his office, or may be distinctive at the meet by the leather satchel over his shoulder. However, if neither of these is apparent, it is up to the mounted follower to seek him out and pay his dues at the meet. Very often as the hunt moves off, the Secretary will go ahead and place himself at the first gateway, and in this way it should be impossible for any non-payer to slip through.

Even more important for a visitor is that he has telephoned the Secretary in advance to ensure that it is permissible for him to hunt on a given day, for in some areas the size of the field (i.e. the mounted followers) has to be restricted.

The Committee

The committee will usually consist of a set number of subscribers and farmers, and will either remain *in situ* indefinitely, or be obliged to retire on a rotational basis after, say, three years. The committee will decide whom to ask to join them on the committee, usually those who have been involved for many years and have the necessary knowledge and enthusiasm.

The chairman is at the helm and, under him, the committee may be responsible for appointing and paying the hunt staff (this task may be undertaken by the Master) and making the major decisions concerning the hunt, such as the price of subscriptions and the days that will be hunted.

The Master

At the head of affairs is the Master, or Masters. They are appointed by the hunt committee, who guarantee them so much money from subscriptions, and it is up to the Master to provide the rest. Sometimes they are appointed only to act for the committee, in other words, not to be responsible for unlimited cash injection. So, although the hunt chairman is actually a most important man, his is a behind-the-scenes role, and it is still the Master who carries the prestige – and the burdens. Even where the committee produces much of the cash, the Master normally has to delve into his own pocket, and sometimes quite deeply.

The Master is a man (or woman) to be respected at all times, and about whom personal prejudices must not be allowed to show. It is an onerous task, with very little thanks or reward, although the position does carry with it undoubted social standing in the rural community.

Not so long ago, the Master was nearly always a landowner. However, today, there is much 'new money' with Masters coming from many different walks of life, and their contributions are welcomed. At one time, farmers were not allowed to go to the hunt ball (a farmers' dance was provided for them instead). Now, many farmers are Masters, their great asset being local knowledge and an ability to understand other farmers' problems when the hunt comes over their land.

Joint Masters

Multiple or joint mastership has become a feature of today which not only eases an individual's financial burden but helps with the work-load, too. It can be that a committee will endeavour to have two gentlemen (or lady) Masters and two farmers.

They are often appointed different areas of the country to look after, being responsible for speaking to the farmers

Fig 24   Three of the Grafton Hunt's five Joint-Masters, 1989. Many hunts ease the burden of the mastership by sharing the load. Left to right: Henry Russell, Tim Brown, and John Busby, all of them farmers.

Fig 25   The Border Foxhounds in Northumberland, with their Joint-Master and huntsman Michael Hedley.

before and frequently after hunting, seeing to the repair of any damage, and the building and maintenance of hunt jumps in their area. One Master may be responsible for overseeing the kennel staff, another the stables and one may be appointed overall executive Master.

Additionally, the Master will be expected to put in an appearance at many social and fund-raising activities. He will be responsible for entertaining farmers and landowners, providing the puppy show's elaborate tea and good-quality prizes for the puppy walkers (those farmers and subscribers who look after a couple of hound puppies for a few months between weaning and their return to kennel with the adult pack of hounds). But whatever their duties (and

many of the subscribers will have no idea of them), it is up to hunt followers to show the Masters deference at all times.

One of hunting's traditions is that the Master is always called 'Master' (even female ones), at least on the first greeting of the day when out hunting. After that, a personal friend may revert to calling him by his Christian name. At the meet, however, it is 'Good morning, Master'; at the end of the day, or even if leaving early, it is 'Good night, Master', regardless of the hour.

If for some reason the Master needs to make his way through the field, the call 'Master, please' should ensure that everyone makes way for him. This latter applies equally to 'Huntsman, please, on your right', or similarly to a whipper-in who is trying to carry out his professional duties and needs to get by in a hurry.

The Amateur Huntsman/Master

Some hunts have an amateur huntsman who may also be Master or Joint Master. As this is a time-consuming job, it is essential that he either has private means or an indulgent boss, or some form of financial backing or subsidy, probably from a hunting well-wisher. This person is likely to be a truly dedicated fox-hunter, totally wrapped up in the sport and his hounds.

Identification

A Master wears a black hunting cap with the ribbons still on at the back. A farmer may also have his cap ribbons free, but a subscriber must sew them up or cut them off. Like most hunting traditions, there is a practical reason for it, in this case one of identification.

The Master has four buttons on his scarlet coat, unless he is also hunting hounds, in which case he has five, as does the professional huntsman whose coat should be square cut. Subscribers should wear a coat with three buttons and well-rounded points. Other hunting dress details are described in Chapter 6.

Field Master

More often than not, one of the Masters also acts as field master, or it may be divided between the Masters according to their particular piece of country or day of the week. Sometimes this will be a separate appointment, given to someone

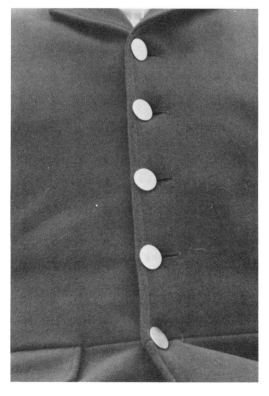

Fig 26   Five buttons for a hunt servant, inscribed with his hunt's initials.

with knowledge of the country and of the sport.

His role is to head the field and to keep it under control – not always an enviable task, especially when hounds are flying and the country ahead is good! But it is imperative that he keeps command. It is he who knows where there is land from which the hunt is banned, he who can recognise a new ley from old grass, and he who will ensure that hounds are not over-ridden. His is a task calling for natural leadership, respect and authority so that, it must be hoped, he does not have to resort to yelling and bawling at members of the field in order to control them.

Fig 27   Hunt staff from far and wide will support their colleagues. Here, at the retirement meet of Bryan Pheasey after 25 years' service with the Bicester (later amalgamated with the Whaddon Chase) are, left to right, John Kennelly (Pytchley), Tom Normington (Grafton), Peter Jones (Pytchley) and Billy Marples (Barlow).

The Huntsman

Except where there is an amateur huntsman, the huntsman is a paid professional hunt servant, very often stemming from a long line of hunt servants. He is also the kennel huntsman (a post which only exists separately where there is an amateur huntsman) who is responsible for kennel management, and probably plays a leading part in hound breeding.

The huntsman's primary role is to provide the sport during the hunting season. It is an art which requires deep knowledge of country lore (probably having been born and bred to it), dedication, patience, skill, tact and diplomacy. He addresses Masters and subscribers as 'Sir' or 'Madam', but the kennel staff beneath him in their turn address the huntsman as 'Sir'.

He becomes well known in the locality and in his own way plays an important part in assisting good hunt relations in the neighbourhood, particularly with farmers. Pay will not be high, but the job

49

will include cottage and perks such as skin money from the carcasses brought in and Christmas boxes from subscribers, traditionally given at the Boxing Day meet.

How he actually hunts his hounds will be described in Chapter 7. Hounds and huntsman share a mutual love, respect and trust in each other, something the new entry (puppies of about a year old at the start of their hunting career) will quickly pick up. They will have been out on daily hound exercise during the summer, walked at first, then accompanied by the staff on bicycles, and finally on horseback to prepare them and get them fit for the coming season.

Whipper-In

The first rung on the ladder towards being a huntsman in the larger hunts which employ two whips, is usually that of second whipper-in. Many of his tasks in the kennel will be of the menial variety. In the hunting field, his task is to round up, or whip in, the straggling hounds, and to assist the huntsman in whatever way he requires.

To him and the first whip (the next step in promotion), the horse is a tool of the trade. Often at this stage their riding experience is limited, but being young men and keen to succeed, they know no fear. Their horses generally have to travel further and faster in carrying out their duties in a day, and so a stout, tough animal is essential.

Amateur Whips

In addition to one or two professional whips, there is often an amateur whip, official or otherwise. In countries where it is essential to have three or four corners of a covert being watched when hounds are put in, it is usual for experienced followers to be sent on a 'point'. This gives the opportunity to play an important role. The sense of anticipation enjoyed by the field waiting to hear the 'Gone away' is heightened for the person on point. He may have the luck to have the fox leave the covert near him and so be in the forefront of the ensuing sport. Conversely, the action may happen at the furthest point away, and he will just have to catch up as best he can.

Gate-Shutters and Fence Menders

One of the unpardonable sins of hunting is for a follower to fail to close a gate to a field containing stock, or to mend a fence should he have the misfortune to break one. Increasingly, two gate-shutters are appointed for each day's hunting. Drawing up the rota from the list of subscribers is one of the Secretary's tasks.

However, this in no way eliminates the follower's responsibilities as stated above. There is no excuse whatever for leaving open a gate to a stock field unless someone behind is within hailing distance. You then shout 'Gate, please', and watch for an acknowledgement before continuing.

It is no use leaving it just because the gate-shutters are on their way. They may be held up repairing an earlier fence or, of course, the field may have split into two or more groups and the gate-shutters can only follow one of them, so they may not be coming that way at all.

If there is only one person coming behind, the next to last one should stay

Fig 28 A gate-shutter (left), equipped for the job.

back with him to help shut the gate or, if necessary, hold the other's horse, or simply prevent the other horse from fretting as it sees the rest galloping away.

The duty gate-shutters for the day will be distinguishable because they are wearing ratcatcher (tweed jacket instead of black, or whatever the hunt's own jacket colour is) and usually copious strands of binder twine attached to the rear of the saddle and hanging down the horse's flanks.

In most packs, the gate-shutters are required to stay out until 3p.m. After that, they are free to go home or to join in with the sport like anyone else, and it is up to those remaining to remember their corporate duties.

Breaking Gates

Some hunts have a rule that whoever has the misfortune to break a gate has to pay for it, usually a fixed sum. This is bad luck if the gate was old and rotten and your horse only just touched it, but a rule is a rule and the payment should be paid graciously. At least there will be a nice new gate for the farmer!

Nothing damages hunting more quickly than for a justifiably irate farmer to find his stock wandering about miles away from where they should be, or trampling a field of corn because one thoughtless rider has failed to secure a gate or patch up a broken fence. It is therefore sensible for every mounted

51

follower to carry a piece of string and a penknife, just in case emergency repairs have to be carried out.

Mending Fences

Some hunts employ fence menders in a paid capacity, who will follow the hunt round in a Land Rover complete with suitable materials for fence mending in that area (usually stakes, rails and, of course, hammer and nails).

The only pack I have ever been with where it did not seem to matter about fence breaking was with the Galway Blazers in the west of Ireland. This is renowned dry-stone-wall country where, dare I say it, the sport seemed to be all jumping orientated, and a massive tourist ego trip for the visiting Americans and Germans who well outnumbered the Irish themselves. It seemed not to matter how much a wall had crumpled, as it was all left to the fence mender (or rather, wall builder) who was never far behind. But to me it did not seem to be the real thing. I should add that it is a good few years since I hunted there, so it may have changed.

Earth Stopper/ Terrier Man

Another role in the hunt, and one the new subscriber is unlikely to be aware of, is that of earth stopper. He is more likely to see the terrier man, or men, carrying a spade in one hand and a terrier under his arm. The Meynell terrier man follows mounted, with his terrier peeping out of a canvas bag strapped to his back!

It is the duty of the earth stopper to block the entrance of a known earth the

Fig 29   The terrier man's work starts when the fox goes to ground.

night before hunting is due in that area, to stop the fox going to ground during the hunt. The man may be paid by the hunt, it may sometimes be undertaken by hunt staff, or very often it will be the farmer himself who sees to it.

The terrier man is used on the day of the hunt if a fox goes to ground and the decision is made either to kill it, with a humane killer, or to bolt it using the terriers. However, if it is felt enough foxes have been accounted for in that area on the day, and the huntsman or Master is anxious to move straight on to another patch, it may be left, subject to the wishes of the local farmer.

Fig 30 *He may cross several fields by foot to reach the earth ...*

Fig 31 *... and he may find himself on his hands and knees to reach it!*

Fig 32 Meynell Hunt terrier man, Greg Mousley, jumping a fence with his terrier in a satchel during a hunt in Derbyshire.

Fig 33   The fence mender's vehicle.

Medical Aid

Some hunts today ensure that their repair vehicle carries with it a stretcher and basic first aid equipment, as well as having someone knowledgeable to deal with serious mishaps. Also, on a strictly informal, non-official basis, there is sometimes a vet and/or doctor among the subscribers and I have yet to come across one who does not willingly and quickly go to help someone in trouble, even if it means forfeiting their own sport in the process. The Heythrop Hunt, I believe, has no fewer than four doctors among its ranks.

6 Etiquette, Behaviour and Children

One of the aspects of hunting that worries the newcomer is the question of etiquette. Yet there is really nothing magical or secret about it, for like most things it is a question of common sense and basic manners. There is a practical reason behind almost all the traditions of hunting, and it is certainly going to help the newcomer if he is aware of most of them before he sets out.

We have already mentioned saying 'Good morning' and 'Good night' to the Master (no matter what the time of day for the latter, and no matter if the Master is female), and this is a custom which keeps respect alive. Another tradition is to ensure you present a Christmas box to the hunt staff at the meet on Boxing Day, an occasion which usually takes place at a major town within the hunt, and is the golden opportunity to 'show the flag' to the general public who love nothing

Fig 34 Boxing Day always draws the crowds – and the tinsel.

more than to pat the hounds and to admire the horsemen and horses. They love the scarlet worn by the hunt servants, male Masters and those subscribers who have been awarded the hunt button.

Hunt Button

The hunt button is awarded to those who have hunted for some time with a given pack, have shown their usefulness and knowledge and are generally acknowledledged to be part and parcel of the hunt. It means that instead of plain black buttons, they are entitled to wear the hunt's own inscribed button (some are illustrated in Fig. 26 and Fig. 35). It also entitles a male subscriber to wear scarlet, if he so wishes. The matter of dress is discussed in fuller detail in Chapter 4.

Fig 35   Hunt buttons – each hunt has its own individual pattern.

Fox and Hound Terminology

Some terminology to remember regarding a fox is: his head is called his mask; the tail is called the brush; his feet are known as pads; his nickname is Charlie or Charles-James. As for hounds, they are never dogs, always hounds; and the tail is called the stern. A tail-hound is one at the back of the pack.

The Holloa

Probably the worst thing you can do as a newcomer, and one that is so easily perpetrated in the excitement of it all, is to yell, 'There he is!' if you see the fox (generally referred to as viewing). Do not say a word or move a muscle. If you yell, the fox will immediately turn round and run back into the covert, possibly straight into the pack of hounds, but certainly thwarting a possibly good hunt.

That is what it is all about – culling the fox population rather than leaving it to multiply out of control to the detriment of other wild life, or to be shot to extermination.

The fox is a hunter, and when it is his turn to be hunted, displays great *sang froid* about the whole affair, very calmly pausing, or lolloping along. Old, weak or injured foxes are done a good service when despatched by hounds. Basically, without hunting, foxes would either proliferate to excess in certain areas (and so many people are pestered by dustbin foxes), or would be wiped out in others by snares, poisoning or shooting by frustrated farmers.

Somebody who does know what to do will holloa at the appropriate moment. The fox then gets a start, hounds tumble out of the covert and race with their heads

Fig 36 Hounds pausing for a refreshing drink during the day.

down as they settle to the line, and only then can the mounted field follow. Remember, it is the hounds who are hunting the fox, and the field who are following the hounds. In this respect it is a spectator sport.

If you find yourself alone and there is no other way that you can let it be known that you have seen the fox, and if you are sure it is the hunted fox (there could be a brace or more about), then you may holloa. However, if one of the hunt officials is within sight, it is a better idea to try just raising your hat (or your whip if you are wearing a chin strap) in the air, pointing in the direction that the fox has gone.

Over-Riding

It is important not to over-ride or get ahead of the hounds. Give them a chance to settle down. In your eagerness to get going, a grand hunt may be spoilt if you distract the hounds. Should you find yourself in a position between where the fox has gone and the hounds are coming, stand still. If you move about, you may foil the line (scent).

How to Behave with Hounds

When hounds come through the field, probably between draws, and you have to get out of their way, move to the side and, most important, turn your horse's head towards the hounds. This should ensure that you do not perpetrate the crime of kicking one. It is also wise to drop the thong of your whip down to ground level as this discourages a hound from coming too close.

If a straggling hound is coming through the field from behind, especially down a narrow ride, it is helpful to call to the person in front of you 'Hound on the right' (or the left), so that he can give it room to come through. It is useful to remember here that hounds are always counted in couples.

Gates and Bridges

There is little more painful than to have a swinging gate catch the point of your knee (except perhaps to be kicked on the knee). If the opening is narrow and cannot be made wider, lift up both your lower legs and pivot them forwards along the line of the saddle, to prevent them being hit. If the gate is a swinger, make sure you do not let it go until you are certain the person behind you can catch hold of it safely. Then do not gallop away until that person has let the next one through, or his horse may get het up.

The same principle applies to bridges. Do not underestimate the lethal nature of bridges. They are nearly always slippery and sometimes have alarming holes in them. You must walk over them and you must stop on the other side until the next rider is over. If you gallop off, you may cause a serious accident to the person who is on the bridge.

Likewise, it is dangerous to gallop through gateways, especially if they are muddy. Underneath that soft mud, slippery concrete may be lurking, or large stones or potholes.

Stock and Cattle Yards

It is important not to disturb farm stock, either inside or outside the farm. In other words, always walk through a farmyard, especially where cattle are yarded, and do not gallop through a flock of sheep or herd of cattle in the fields however hard hounds are running. Give them a wide berth. The sheep may well be in-lamb ewes.

Wherever you go, and no matter how exciting the hunt, do thank anybody who holds open a gate, or whoever is in a farmyard. It could well be the farmer, and a smile and a word of thanks can make all the difference to the hunt being allowed on his land.

Remember, it is at all times by courtesy of the farmers and landowners that you may enjoy the privilege of riding over their property and be in the position to see, and be a part of, our wonderful countryside.

Fig 37 Do not forget to greet the farmer as you ride through his yard or across his land.

Kicking

If you ride a horse that is known to kick, you must tie a red ribbon to his tail and you must take all precautions to prevent him getting in range of other horses, including staying at the rear of the field. If you know little or nothing about the horse, it is a good idea to tie a green ribbon to his tail, especially if he is young and/or novice. This is simply an indication that he is not yet an experienced hunter and so you are not sure what his reactions will be.

If you find yourself on a horse who kicks, you must put one hand behind your back, spread palm outermost, when you are in a confined space with other riders, such as going through a gateway or down a narrow ride.

Kicking is, however, a two-sided affair. Except for out-and-out kickers, who simply should not be brought out hunting, there is the point that to be kicked, a person usually will have got himself within kicking range. However, on one occasion my innocent horse was kicked in the middle of a large arable field by a fractious three year old who swung round, backed at alarming speed, and kicked before there was any chance of getting out of the way.

The way people crowd at gateways, it is surprising that more are not kicked out hunting. You should endeavour to keep out of range, and make sure that you

Fig 38 A red ribbon tied round a horse's tail indicates that he is a kicker, or a horse that it is thought may kick.

Fig 39   This hand signal means 'Beware – this horse may kick.'

do so if you see someone put a hand behind his back.

Even at the end of a long day, a kicker may still kick (other horses will also, because they are uncomfortable with sweat), so they must still be given a wide berth.

Do not ride on people's heels. It is ill-mannered and irresponsible, and you have only yourself to blame if you are kicked.

Helping Your Horse

At the end of a good run, with horses steaming and the thrill of it glowing, dismount your horse, lead him away from the crowd and turn his face towards the breeze. This will help him get his breath back.

During a good run, try to pick your ground where possible. For instance, when crossing plough, a water-filled furrow will be easier on him. Do not give him a long drink, but short swallows from a trough during the day should do no harm.

Neither Brag nor Grumble

It may be as well not to brag about what you have jumped; after all, it is the horse who has done the jumping, not you, and how often does pride come before a fall? Mind you, it is nice to praise your horse and feel full of him for his prowess. By

61

Fig 40   Plastered with mud – quite a contrast to the immaculate
turn-out at the meet.

Fig 41   Many countries have to face up and adapt to increasing
amounts of plough.

the same token, do not criticize your Master or huntsman. They know a lot more about the job than you, but it is very easy to become a 'grandstand jockey'.

The huntsman usually has a canny idea of where the fox has gone. Do not follow him round when he is making his cast, keep quiet and still. Use your eyes and ears, learn those tell-tale signs such as the sheep moving in a distant field or birds flying out of the covert. Within moments, you may see the fox slip out. Watch the hounds hit off the line – it will bring a quiet pleasure that all those chattering coffee housers missed. Many of them probably also missed that awakened owl flying to a new perch, or the heron flapping lazily by the brook. Do not grumble when the scent is bad. More boloney is talked about scenting conditions than anything else!

Traffic

It is essential at all times to allow the traffic through as quickly and with as little fuss as possible. Nothing damages the image of hunting more quickly than blocking roads so that through traffic cannot pass. Be extra courteous at all times – it might make all the difference. Although you have every right to be on the road, you do not own it and you most certainly do not have the right to block it or cause a hazard.

It is as well to remember that roads are death-traps, not only because of traffic but because of slippery, hard tarmacadam. More serious accidents arise out of falls on the road than are caused by jumping over the biggest of fences (*see* page 100).

Jumping

Jumping out hunting will be looked at in closer detail in Chapter 8. Under etiquette, though, it is essential: (i) to keep a straight line approaching a fence, (ii) not to 'queue barge', and (iii) if you have a refusal, get out of the way quickly and let others go. If hounds are running and the place is narrow, it is very unfair on those waiting behind if you keep having a go instead of letting others try. Finally, do not 'skylark' and do not jump going home.

Children

All the foregoing applies equally to children, and there are a few other points for them as well.

In most hunts, young children will be charged a small fee, usually well within pocket-money limits, while those on a leading rein will normally be free. Young people between the age of eighteen and twenty-one will normally be charged a percentage of the adult subscription, probably about one-third, and will also be expected to pay field money.

The Safe Pony

There is nothing worse than to see a child frightened to death as his pony gallops out of control. A 'bomb-proof' pony at home can all too easily transform into a little devil out hunting. It is imperative that an adult accompanies a child out hunting for the first time. Some hunts, wisely, insist on it up to a certain age, and some require all children to carry identification.

Fig 42   *A young rider and pony covered in mud after a spectacular fall on a very wet day.*

Fig 43   Never too young.

Fig 44   Nina (with belly clip) and George. A safe pony is of paramount importance to a child starting to hunt.

The Children's Meet

The annual children's or Pony Club meet is a keenly anticipated occasion. No adults come other than those accompanying children or one or two assistants. This is the day when a few of the older children will be asked to accompany the hunt servants and Field Master, a wonderful educational experience when the art of hunting can be learnt at first hand. Control may not be at its peak so it is best to start off a small child at a quiet meet.

Remember not to bring out a young child for too long as he may get bored, cold, hungry and tired. It is far better to give him a quiet introduction and so get him longing for the next time. Make sure he wears warm clothes, takes a pair of gloves, and at least a bar of chocolate in his pocket. Finally, you should ensure that your child is well-mannered: he should always be ready to nip off his pony to open a gate or offer assistance in any way – and he must not barge about! Nor must adults for that matter.

7 The Hunt

The hunt is what it's all about, so let's get on with explaining what happens without further ado. We have already talked about how to prepare for it, so now we shall whet the appetite a little bit more...

The Meet

It is no accident that the hunt servants and the vast majority of followers look smart at the meet, for they or their staff will have been up early, grooming and plaiting horses, cleaning tack, brushing clothes and polishing boots. This is how it should be as keeping up standards can never be a bad thing.

The mounted and foot followers foregather at the appointed place and time. Those with horses should take care not to park on village greens or in front of gateways, and should hack for at least

Fig 45   The whip leads the hounds to the meet.

Fig 46   The meet.

half a mile to get the horse's back down and to let him settle – that is the theory, anyway. 'Walk a mile, trot a mile, and do what you like after'. In other words, warm your horse up first before expecting him to gallop or jump.

Friends and the Master are greeted, the Secretary paid, a kicker is kept out of the way, and a stirrup cup is very likely taken (unless the meet is at a remote cross-roads). There is a keen sense of anticipation, especially if those 'red wine' experts declare scent is sure to be good. One of the hardest things to decribe are the various sounds made on the horn, but on leaving the meet it is most likely to be a short toot, just a signal to make way for the hounds moving off.

Pecking Order

The rest follow in a certain informal pecking order. Obviously the Field Master is at the head, and probably with him will be any joint Masters. The Secretary will be on hand, ready to position himself at the first convenient gateway in order to collect any late caps, and then there will be the hunt stalwarts who have hunted with the pack for many seasons.

The Draw

Either as the first draw is reached or a little before, one or two of the regulars will be sent on ahead. They will know

Fig 47   Un-boxing should be off the road if possible, and at
least half a mile from the meet.

Fig 48   Ready for the day – double bridle, plaited mane and tail.

Fig 49   Hacking on.

Fig 50   Hounds unloading.

the lie of the land well and will know just where to position themselves around the covert to keep watch, 'on point' as it is known.

When they, plus the whipper-in, are in position, the huntsman will put the hounds into covert to 'draw' it (look for the fox by nose). Until then, they have been held together as a pack, sterns waving, eagerness showing all over their faces, but not daring to go ahead until they have heard their huntsman's command. Then with a 'Lieu in there' and probably a wave of the hand and perhaps a sound on the horn, in they will go, searching for the one scent they are bred and trained to hunt – the distinctive smell of a fox.

The amount of horn and voice heard will vary both between huntsmen and terrain. If it is very wooded, a considerable amount of vocal encouragement will be needed. It is no good the huntsman getting off to a good hunt if the field have not heard anything. Where there is a small covert being drawn, however, not very much noise will be needed, as everyone should be able both to see and hear.

Some of the huntsman's encouraging terms will be 'Yip, try, try-y-y' when drawing; 'wind 'im in there' when the fox is to ground; 'Get away on to 'im' and 'Cope for'ard' to the stragglers; and 'On, on, on' when away on a hunt. At a kill, it will be 'Whoo-whoop'.

Fig 51   Hacking to covert.

The Field

The Field Master will have the field held together at one corner of the covert, probably on the side where he least wants the fox to go, either because the country is better for riding across the other way, or because of the wishes of the local farmers. A number of people by now will be catching up on the week's gossip with their friends, but many will be alert, looking and listening.

The Find

All of a sudden there will be a whimper from one of the hounds, and a good many of the field will sit up and take notice. The hound is joined by another, then another, and their sound becomes increasingly more positive and excited. They are 'giving tongue'.

The huntsman calls encouragement and it is imperative that the field continues to stay quiet and still. As the hounds crash through the undergrowth, their music is one of the most exhilarating sounds that you can imagine. Suddenly it all goes quiet. For some reason, they can no longer smell their quarry. The huntsman gives them time to work it out for themselves and, just at that moment there comes a clear, long holloa from the far end of the wood. Charlie has left.

71

Fig 52   On the move.

Gone Away

Now comes the most exciting, doubling notes on the horn, 'Gone away', and once more hounds are in full cry. They stream out of the covert, the whipper-in rounds up any stragglers until they are 'all on', and the Field Master sets off in pursuit. The hunt, as far as the mounted field is concerned, has begun.

It may be brief, it may be circular, the scent may prove difficult in the open (out of the wood), or it may turn into the hunt of the season. Like fishing, it is the sense of the unknown, the anticipation, which adds to the excitement. There is nothing like a good hunt early in the day, even if it proves only to be a short, sharp one, to get the adrenalin going. There have been some nice fences, the going is not too bad, and a good number of people are still right up there.

The Check and the Cast

The hounds then check, that is, they have lost the scent. You must wait patiently while they fan out of their own accord trying to pick it up again.

If they are struggling, the huntsman will call them up and cast them where he thinks the fox has most likely gone. Or there may be a holloa in the distance where a foot follower has seen the hunted fox slip by. The huntsman then blows a series of short notes on his horn, encouraging the hounds to follow him and conveying the sense of urgency.

The fox may have tried to foil the scent by going through a field of sheep or cattle, or by rolling in some dung or swimming through a river. Did you not see those sheep moving and huddling together in the distance, or all those birds flying out of that wood in the same direction?

Going to Ground

The fox may go to ground. The huntsman blows a long-drawn-out sound to indicate this. Now the earth stopper's role comes into its own for, if he has done his job, the fox will find the entrance blocked and will have to continue on his way.

Fig 53   Gone to ground! The Cattistock Hunt.

Fig 54 Marking to ground.

Fig 55 Gone to ground.

Sometimes, however, the area will be too thick for the earth stopper to have found all the holes, or there may be a previously unknown drain, or a heap of round straw bales (a favourite modern refuge for foxes), or the fox may have run so far out of the anticipated territory that earth stopping will not have been done.

The End of a Hunt

If the fox has found a safe refuge, this may signal the end of the hunt, when the fox is 'given best', or alternatively the terriers and the terrier men with spades may be called for.

If it is particularly important that the fox is killed, he will be forced to the entrance and shot between the eyes, but sometimes he will be allowed to bolt. Hounds are held back until he has had a start (when he has been given 'law') and then the hunt resumes.

The hunt may end with the fox simply giving hounds the slip, perhaps because of poor scent or through his cunning; or hounds may have to be called off because of failing light or because the hunt has been requested to avoid the ground ahead on that day; or the fox may be killed 'on top', that is, above ground or 'in the open', when the huntsman will blow a tremolo on the horn.

Fig 56 The kill.

75

However he is killed, it is highly unlikely that the mounted followers will have seen it, and they are likely to be fulsome in their praise of a 'good' fox.

The Point

The hunt may have lasted only as far as one field (or even less if the fox is killed inside the wood), or it may have run over many miles, producing a fabulous 'point' over as fine a piece of country as can be found anywhere. It may be one of those 'red-letter days' which will be talked about with fond remembrance for years to come.

The point is the distance as the crow flies between the start of a hunt and where it ends. Therefore, if the hunt is circular, there may be virtually no point at all, but if you have got behind a travelling dog fox (one that was far out of his normal terrain the night before in search of a vixen) and he 'takes you home', you could have a splendid point.

A six-mile point, for instance, is a very fair distance, especially as the mounted followers are likely to have gone a good many miles further themselves, due to the terrain, etc. On some days, when scent is high and all the other conditions are just right, hounds may be flying all day and the followers will enjoy the greatest thrill, challenge and excitement.

The Blank Day

By contrast, the very next day could have nothing going right, and occasionally there will even be a blank day, no matter how much homework has been put into the day's sport beforehand.

A blank day is when no fox is found all day. The first covert is drawn blank, the huntsman blows hounds out of covert with a slow, mournful note and, with a certain amount of disappointment, the field moves on to the next draw. This is drawn blank, too, but the next one is a certain find. Sadly, Charlie is not at home there, either. And so it goes on, throughout the day, until home is blown and disappointed hounds are loaded into the trailer, while the remaining faithful followers head home.

It should be pointed out that hunting can be extremely cold, wet, tiring and, yes, boring to even the most ardent follower. It may snow, sleet, hail, pour with rain and blow a gale while the foxes may all be sensibly under ground!

Evening Hunt

On the other hand, it is often these faithful few who enjoy the magic of a splendid evening hunt. Come about 3 p.m., with the sun sinking, the temperature dropping and all but the die-hard followers gone home, scent can improve dramatically, an outlying fox may be found in a hedgerow, and a splendid run can follow. How welcome is the warm stable and mash for the horse and the hot bath and whisky for the human after a day like this!

Cub-Hunting

There is a period of cub-hunting in the autumn before the Opening Meet (traditionally the first week in November but often now held in mid-October due to changing farming methods, meaning hunting ends earlier in the spring than it

Fig 57 Hunting in the rain.

Fig 58 Relaxing after a morning's cub-hunting.

Fig 59   Fox cubs at play.

*Fig 60   Cub-hunting in the early mist, crossing the stubble
before it has been ploughed and sown to winter wheat. The
followers wear ratcatcher.*

Fig 61   The annual hunt puppy show is a summer social function, at which the young entry are judged, and the puppy-walkers thanked.

used to). Cub-hunting (often known as cubbing) takes place in the early morning, usually a lovely time of day. The cubs by this time are full-grown foxes who are still living in litters. These need to be dispersed, otherwise there may be too many foxes living together. This can result in too little food to go round which in turn will make them more likely to start invading a farmer's poultry or, in the spring, taking new born lambs. Cub-hunting culls the weaker foxes, leaving the stronger ones with enough territory in which to establish themselves.

During cub-hunting, the coverts are held up; that is, the riders and foot followers spread out around the covert. It is the one time you will try to head a fox back into the covert, growling 'Ay, ay Charlie' and slapping the side of your saddle with your whip. It is also the time when the young entry (the previous year's hound puppies) are entered, learning from their elders and huntsman what is expected of them.

If a fox goes away, it is likely to be an old one who knows the ropes and, as the object is to split up litters, hounds will be stopped from hunting it. Sometimes, towards the end of October, hounds will be allowed to hunt in the open, while there are some areas, such as Exmoor, not suitable for cub-hunting at all.

Traditionally, you may only come out cub-hunting by courtesy of the Master and so you should ask his or the Secretary's permission first. Dress is more informal. You should wear ratcatcher (a tweed coat and a tweed or spotted hunting tie).

8 Jumping and Falls

One of the main reasons the vast majority of people hunt is for the thrill of jumping. This is a fact of life, whether or not purists approve of it. It is, therefore, just as important for the novice to know how to go about jumping, or equally how not to, as it is to cope with falls.

Jumping in General

In general, do not hang on to your horse's head and above all do not jab him in the mouth. Learn how to slip your reins by just opening your fingers a little and letting the reins slip through until the horse's neck is at full stretch. Then take full hold of them again and do not drop them! If you get left behind on a jump, you may give your horse a nasty bump in the saddle, but if you have learnt how to slip your reins at least you should avoid giving him a jab in the mouth. Nothing turns a good jumper into a habitual refuser quicker than these two things, and it is a crying shame to see.

At the same time, learn how to lean back from the waist and to put your lower legs forward, because if you always lean forward, going with your

Fig 62   An old-fashioned hunting seat.

Fig 63   A forward seat.

horse showjumping style, there are going to be occasions when you will keep on going right over his head and end up on the floor.

You will feel when everything is going right and you can go with your horse, but if you are in a mess, lean back, sit tight and slip the reins. Try to keep your centre of gravity in the right position when taking off and landing. It is something that becomes instinctive and, like learning to rise to the trot or to ride a bicycle, is something that once learnt is never forgotten.

Do not fall into the trap of jumping beside an open gateway. Even a perfect horse may feel too tempted to go for the gap and trouble may follow. Do not skylark but do enjoy yourself. Always remember you may want to save your

horse for a good thing at the end of the day.

Generally, do not jump if hounds are not running unless: (i) it is the easier way, (ii) the field master does so, (iii) it is a poor jumping country so any jump is welcome, or (iv) the farmer whose land you are on positively encourages it (which may be the situation if he is out on the hunt himself). Remember, also, that the neighbouring farmer may discourage it, and do you know where the boundary is? Most important of all, keep your eye on the Field Master; be guided by him.

It is seldom the 'thrusters', incidentally, who do the damage out hunting, but their hangers-on. It is at the back of the field that probably the most damage of all is done, as a day gate-shutting testifies. One wonders if some of the

Fig 64   A first-class illustration of why you should not jump beside an open gate.

followers are hunting at all! However, as long as they report or, better still, mend any damage, and do not ride on crops or places that are not permitted, if they are enjoying themselves, then all well and good.

It is not always the case that the thrusters are the backbone of the hunt (though it is unlikely to be the tail-enders either), but the wily older person with a love and knowledge of country lore, using both his eyes and ears, and generally being in the right place at the right time, up with hounds at the end of a run, but without perhaps having jumped a fence at all.

It has been made clear already that there is seldom any need to jump. There fore, the person who does not want to can always find a way round the obstacle. Discretion, too, should play the better part of valour, and should an enormous fence be looming that you do not feel ready for or, more important, that your horse is patently not capable of, then forget it. Go round or find a smaller one. You will not be on your own in doing this. Only very rarely does a rider get left behind on his own because his horse will not jump.

Fig 65   Queueing for a hunt jump.

Types of Jump

Hunt Jumps and Tiger Traps

Most hunts have hunt jumps, in the form of upright rails or tiger traps, and these are well within the capabilities of most horses and riders. They are usually located in places regularly used through-out the season, and are generally taken in single file or, at the most, two abreast.

This causes two problems: queueing and poached ground. There is nothing more annoying than the queue barger, but every hunt has one (probably several). Two wrongs do not make a right, however, and you really must wait your turn, however annoying it is to have

someone cut in from behind you. What almost invariably happens is that the remaining riders push up ever closer to the jump, so that in the end horses are trying to jump it off their hocks from about two paces, and then they start refusing, causing more congestion and irritation.

A fine example of a hunt which did not do this was the Albrighton Woodland which, on my visit there, had everyone holding back far enough and waiting their turn. As a result, everyone got over and away more quickly and smoothly than in many other places.

It is an unwritten rule that should your horse refuse in a situation like this, you must not hold up people further by

Fig 66 Note here how the reins have been slipped to avoid pulling on the horse's mouth and the lower leg put forward to help balance.

trying again, but must go back and wait your next turn. It is also at this sort of place that there is the danger of kicking. Not only are people bunching up too closely, but the horses will have seen the jump ahead and some, in their excitement, may kick out or swing their quarters around which can cause quite a hefty bump.

Once it is your turn to go, point your horse straight at the fence, not at an angle, make sure he has seen it and give a good kick, especially if the ground is heavy. Try to go 'with' him over the fence, and try to make it a habit to pat him when you are safely over and on your way again. As with humans, a please or thank you never goes amiss and costs nothing.

Another common form of hunt jump is the tiger trap. Instead of upright rails, the rails are sloped on both sides, usually so that the base can spread out over a ditch. The slope makes them inviting to jump, but the ditch staring out from beneath often makes horses spook, and therefore refuse. Keep hold of your horse's head and give him a really good kick so that he knows you mean business.

Fig 67   Hounds have been told to stay back whilst their huntsman jumps.

I had one day in the shires jumping big hedges beautifully. The smallest fence of the day was a tiger trap, and beyond it a field of heavy plough. My intelligent horse saw the deep ground beyond (something he hated) and refused point blank to jump the fence, no matter that it was half the height of what he had just been jumping with ease.

Banks

The first time you meet a steep bank or find you have to negotiate a yawning ditch can be an awesome moment. In fact, it is probably something you will never really relish, unless you hunt a lot in Ireland, and that's a different matter . . .

The thing to remember about a bank is to go straight down it, like the Hickstead Derby bank. If you go sideways, hoping to alleviate the gradient, it is far more likely that the horse will slip. Slip your reins, maintaining light contact with the horse's mouth, and lean back from the waist. It is all about balance, as in skiing or cycling, and a certain finesse. Do not have your hands wooden, but squeeze on the reins and sit tight, encouraging your horse to take small, walking steps.

For going up a steep bank you must lean forward and, if necessary, virtually wrap your arms around your horse's neck. Do not pull tightly on the reins, instead just give him his head; do not lean back or you run the danger of pulling him over backwards.

For banks that want jumping, as opposed to walking up or down, again it is important to go with your horse, leaning slightly forward, and not pulling him off balance in any way.

Ditches

Various parts of the country have ditches, not only in Ireland but also especially in East Anglia. My father loves recounting the story against himself of the time he approached a wide ditch in the middle of a field in Sussex, an unusual occurrence in that part of the world.

'Don't worry, my horse is Irish and knows how to jump ditches,' he cried as he set off at a gallop. The mare certainly

Fig 68 Dr Robert Fountain jumping a ditch in Lincolnshire with the Burton Hunt.

Fig 69   Setting off for a day's hunting in Ireland.

saddle, lean forward a little from the waist, shoot the lower legs forward, loosen the reins and hold on to the neck strap. This will avoid pulling on the horse's mouth, and thus possibly causing him to land short into the ditch.

Gates

Some hunts charge for a broken gate. You can break rails with impunity (though this is not advisable) but if you tap the rotten top rail of an old farm gate, it can cost quite a bit to buy a spanking new gate for the farmer. Whether or not it was either your own or your horse's fault is immaterial. You must pay up with good grace.

Years ago, hunting with the Eridge, my father's horse hit a gate and he fell off, his hat crunching down on his nose which promptly blew up like an orange.

'Have you broken it?' enquired the concerned lady Master.

'I don't think so, but it's very painful,' my father replied, holding up a handkerchief.

'I didn't mean your nose,' came back the quick reply. 'Is the gate broken?'

'Hairy' Places

These are not jumps as such, but nevertheless obstacles to be negotiated, coming in all shapes and sizes. A desperately overgrown ride (track) can be several hundred yards long, and this is the time when you will wish you had a small horse! Crouch as low over your horse's neck as you can, and keep your eyes as near to closed as possible. Your horse will almost certainly obligingly follow the one ahead of him, but do not let him go fast. You must keep your wits about you.

did know how to jump a ditch but only from a standstill. As she suddenly saw the obstacle, she put on all the brakes, catapulting my father over her head. As he lay prostrate in the bottom already laughing, the mare laughed back, then calmly popped over the ditch and cantered off.

No matter how big the ditches in Ireland, the horses come to a virtual standstill and then leap. It is an extremely uncomfortable manoeuvre and can be very unseating (it was how my young son was christened in the hunting field, in spite of a neck strap). The best way to cope is to sit plumb in the middle of the

Fig 70   Breaking a gate with the Glamorgan Hunt.

Fig 71   A 'hairy' place.

Hold up one arm with your whip in it to try to clear a way and protect your face at the same time.

A tall, thin hedge that needs to be pushed through rather than jumped over requires a certain amount of boldness from your horse. Face him at it exactly where you want to go, squeeze him on and, if necessary, slap him down the shoulder and urge him vocally to 'Go on!'

When you negotiate a 'hairy' place on top of a bank, you are quite likely to have your eyes closed. If the horse jumps off and gallops straight on you will probably be all right but if, as happened to me on my first visit to the Meath in Ireland, your horse sees hounds running left or right and cleverly turns on landing to follow them, you are most likely to find yourself going straight on and sitting on the turf.

Low Branches

It is easy to be swept off by a low branch, as I recall when jumping a small stream only to have my horse duck under a branch straight ahead and leaving me hanging Tarzan-like from my arms, having very quickly kicked my feet free of the stirrup irons. Because I had given him his head over the stream, I had not had the time to shorten the reins in order to turn or stop him on landing!

When riding past a protruding branch and having to hold it out of your way, try to ensure that you do not let go of it just as someone is coming. It will give either him or his horse a nasty smack in the face. Whippy saplings you must be especially careful of, because they can do lasting damage to the eyes, and at best are extremely painful.

Rivers and Bogs

If you are wading a deep river, remember to lift your legs up to avoid getting your boots full of water. Should your horse flounder, remain sitting as calmly as possible, helping him all you can. Do not bale out. If the water is out of his depth, and you are off him, he will instinctively use you as a lever to get himself out – and to be fully submerged with half a ton of horse on top of you is exceedingly frightening, to say nothing of the damage a shod hoof can do to your body even under water.

If you are crossing a stream with steep banks, see that it is safe first, but then try to be among the early ones to cross. Banks have a habit of giving way the more they are trodden on. The same applies to crossing boggy patches as the bog gets deeper and deeper the more it is ploughed through. Self-preservation is the name of the game, as long as you do not barge or push people out of your way. Again, sit in the middle of the saddle and make things as easy for your horse as you can. If you get left behind and pull on his mouth as he plunges through, it could be very precarious.

Hedges

Oh, the joy of a grass country, free of wire, with well-grown hedges abounding! And how comparatively rare nowadays to find them, with such sweeping changes having taken place in agriculture since the war.

Some packs have no hedges, in others one or two will be jumped in a whole season. Some will have one or two a day, but a few will be jumping them all day, with hounds streaming in front and you

Fig 72   Mrs John Whittall leading the way through the Hughley Brook, with the South Shropshire Hunt.

*Fig 73   Mrs Rosemary Samworth jumping a cut and laid
hedge with the Cottesmore Hunt.*

watching for a left or right swing, knowing you can follow course in safety.

In the shires, while hounds are in covert, riders will be eyeing up the lie of the land. The fox goes away, and the generous Field Master will say 'Help yourselves, gentlemen', and off stream the intrepid riders, taking their own line and sharing the greatest thrill with their mounts and each other.

There are some very important rules about this type of jumping, first and foremost of which is that you must ride straight into the fence. If you go at an angle, you run the risk of knocking into and bringing down a rider alongside who has correctly kept to his own line.

Equally, do not ride immediately in someone's pocket. That is, do not go right behind him because if he falls you will inevitably land on top of him – an unnecessary fall for you and probably causing worse damage to the other than might have been.

While it is a good idea to follow a known pilot in your early outings, you must not be that close to him. But if you observe, you can learn. If you see him 'wellying on' at what looks a fairly easy fence, you may be sure he knows there is a big ditch on the landing side, so if you are to avoid landing in the ditch, you must kick on yourself. There are an awful lot of follow-my-leaders out hunting. It is amazing how often everyone will follow each other in line over a hedge, just as if it was a narrow rail, instead of spreading out and jumping in line abreast.

Choose the point at which you are going to jump and stick to it. This way you communicate your intention to your horse. Do not dither just because you are spoilt for choice with a nice wide hedge. Also, do not choose the easiest bit such as the thinnest spot, because a horse will often make a hash of it. Instead, go for the blackest bit. It will make him jump more boldly, and this will pay off not only for the feel it gives you, but especially if there is a ditch on the landing side. By jumping it well, he will clear the ditch in his stride, but if he has gone scrappily through a thin bit, the chances are he will land in the ditch.

Horses often do not like the look of a ditch on the take-off side of a fence. The answer is to ride really boldly into it yourself, kick on, throw your heart over and the horse should follow (but not always: once in a while, you may find you have sailed over but that your horse is still firmly implanted at take-off point).

By and large, hedges can be taken much faster than other fences, flying on, while fixed obstacles should be taken more deliberately and collectedly. However, with hounds flying and a keyed-up cracking horse beneath you, it is surprising at what speed you may find yourself tackling some of the solid obstacles, too. Generally, though, the more solid and high a fence, the more deliberately it should be taken, maintaining contact and impulsion. This is especially important if the take-off is deep.

A bullfinch is a very high hedge with the top few feet of thin and spindly growth which the horse will have to jump through rather than over.

Walls

The wall countries of western Ireland are famous. The enclosures are small, therefore the walls are many. They are generally fairly small and built of dry stone so they crumble easily upon being hit, meaning serious falls or injuries are rare.

Fig 74   A 'bullfinch' in Co. Limerick.

Fig 75   A wall in Gloucestershire. Mr Richard Sumner, show-jumper and Joint-Master of the Heythrop Hunt.

Wall countries in England include those in the Cotswolds, like the Beaufort, Cotswold and North Cotswold, in the High Peak area of Derbyshire with the Meynell and South Staffs, and further north still in Northumberland, in the Tynedale area.

Walls do want jumping fairly carefully, especially the fixed type and higher ones. A horse will soon adapt, but a big knee is a frequent result of a horse hitting a wall, a blemish which invariably takes a long time to disappear, if ever.

However, one of the best days I have had was with the Beaufort when hounds were running so fast that in order to keep up with them there could be no question of jumping the walls slowly. I was pleased with my horse's team chase experience that day!

Wire

Generally speaking, you will not be jumping wire, but if you know your horse can, there are times when you will

Fig 76   The Duke of Beaufort's hunt, moving off from a meet at Badminton House.

Fig 77   Jumping neatly over hunt rails – not over the wire.

be at a distinct advantage. In New Zealand, wire is regularly jumped and certain British packs have a lot. I remember it often being jumped in the East Kent country.

The way I teach a horse to jump wire is to walk up to it first, lean forward and tap the wire with my stick underneath the horse's nose. Unless the sun is shining straight at him, it should then be safe to go back a few paces and pop over it. Alternatively, you can spread a jacket over it, but this is time consuming (and it is when hounds are running that you will want to be saving time by jumping wire), to say nothing of the damage that can be done to an expensive jacket.

I once saw a horse go head over heels when faced with a strand of wire hung across an open gateway. His rider made him gallop flat out and it was perfectly obvious that the horse never saw the wire at all and was literally tripped up. But when I first jumped wire on my palomino, I knew the horse so well by that stage – his blood was up with hounds running – and the friend I was with jumped it first. Sunny and I flew over without hesitation. The pair of us then had the thrill of being alone with hounds in full cry while the rest of the field sought a way round that must have been fully half a mile further.

Drop Fences

Over a drop fence a horse needs to find a fifth leg. A drop fence is when the landing side is considerably lower than the take-off side, and to jump one successfully provides a great sensation as you fly through the air.

At the Cattistock one year, we approached a fairly small-looking hedge with some stone wall in it. Several regulars went higher up but we visitors followed the Field Master who had a quiet smile on his face. The drop was far and away the biggest I have ever jumped and, as several riders came down, the rest all turned away. It was certainly a fence that still gets talked about when the whisky is flowing!

Marker Boards In some hunt countries, marker boards are placed in a fence, half painted red, the other half white. The white will usually be facing the end of the fence line and indicates that that part of the fence is free of wire and safe to jump. The line of fence going on from the red side warns that from that point on it is not safe to jump, usually because of wire.

Falls

The one sure thing about hunting is that if you 'have a cut', there are going to be times when you have a fall. From the vast majority of them you will pick yourself up unscathed, muddy perhaps, with hurt pride possibly. Falls on the flat probably occur just as frequently, and those on the road are without doubt the most dangerous of all.

It is quite easy to be refused off, especially if you have 'thrown your heart over' but your horse has failed to follow, and occasionally your horse may come down at a big hedge if he has met it all wrong. This will often be a light fall, as you have come down with your horse instead of falling through the air from a considerable height. The biggest danger then comes from contact with your horse rather than with the ground, so try to get yourself clear. If you can, keep hold of the reins, but do not do so if your horse is galloping, because the wrench will cause him to spin round so abruptly that he can all too easily damage a tendon. Also, his legs may get caught up in your body, and it is your body which will come off second best.

If you have a flying fall, try to roll yourself into a ball on landing. If you feel hurt, do not try the heroics by immediately attempting to rise. Give yourself a few moments, regain your breath and, if necessary, keep your head down. Several hunts nowadays carry a stretcher in the fence-mender's vehicle and may have instructed that man with some first-aid measures, too, which is to be welcomed.

Many hunts have doctors or vets among their subscribers and, although not obliged to, their human kindness makes it almost certain they will help when needed.

If someone is on the ground in front of you, do not jump and run the risk of landing on him. If there is other help on hand on the landing side, simply find another way round, or wait until the way is clear. If the faller is alone, hand your horse to someone else and climb over to his assistance.

If your horse is down, he may be winded. Do not immediately try to get him to his feet but give him a few

Fig 78   A crashing fall over a hedge with the Heythrop Hunt.

moments to recover his breath. Get his saddle off, or at least undo his girth, but be careful to avoid flailing legs as you do so. If he is struggling, sitting on his head will stop him. If he is stuck in a ditch, it may require further assistance to get him out, such as ropes or even a tractor. Very often your horse will walk away none the worse for wear from either of these worrying situations.

Falls on the Flat

A fall on the flat is always an unpleasant experience, not least because it will usually be totally unexpected, and also because it may well be at speed. The best way of avoiding one is always to keep your horse balanced and on the bit, even when faced with a lovely large field to gallop across. Try to make sure you can control him, especially on corners, or he may easily slip up. Slow him up and try to ensure he is on the right leg.

Likewise, slow up over slippery bridges, walk over them and wait for the following person before galloping off, so that his horse does not get keyed up while on the hazard. The same applies to rocky, muddy gateways and concrete drives.

Falls on the Road

This is by far and away the worst type of fall and, I am afraid, can quite literally be fatal. Again, balance and a slow speed are paramount, no matter how fast hounds are running. If the tarmac is shiny it is lethal. Deaths usually occur through head injuries (headwear is discussed on page 28). Suffice to say, ignore those dyed-in-the-wool old-timers who insist on top hats or no chin straps, and instead wear a safe hat.

Be especially careful going downhill and round corners on the road. Use a verge where possible, but remember the possibility of your horse shying out into the road and also keep your eyes peeled for hazards such as bottles and tins discarded in the grass, and ditches crossing the verge. The best compromise may be to ride down the edge of the road where the surface is often rougher.

Do not ride over drain covers. They are invariably slippery and if they are either loose or, worse still, broken, a terrible fall will result.

Maintain contact with your horse's mouth at all times, talk to him if it helps, and be careful!

9 The Hunting Morning and Evening

Time never passes more quickly than when preparing on a hunting morning (other than when you are enjoying a flying hunt). It is no good, however much time you think you have got when getting ready to go, it will disappear quicker than you had imagined – and then the telephone goes, or the dog is sick, or a button comes off.

This chapter should, therefore, begin the night before when you need to set out your hunting clothes; having ironed your tie, given a final polish to your boots and a final brush to your jacket, and made sure you have got sufficient fuel in your vehicle.

Timing

Work out your timing backwards from 11 a.m. (assuming that is the time of the meet). Make sure you know how far away the meet is, and have a good idea in your mind whereabouts you intend to unbox. Leave enough time for parking and try to avoid the tendency of getting closer than half a mile. Do not park in gateways or on village greens nor on the opposite side of the road to another vehicle. Check there is room for the milk tanker to get through. Try to park downhill and make sure you do not get stuck – grass that is hard with frost in the morning may soon be soft once it has thawed!

Keep enough time for taking off rugs, tightening the girth, mounting, and also for putting on your jacket, cap and boots. I always wear a quilted jacket while driving (which is nice to put on when returning home) and I do not drive in hunting boots because: (i) the soles may be slippery on the pedals, (ii) I want to prevent wearing down the heels, and (iii) they are not too comfortable, having been designed for riding, not for walking or driving.

If you are hacking, you need only allow the time it takes to ride there. A fit horse, walking and trotting on, should average six miles per hour.

Food

Let us assume you are doing your own horse, without help. You will probably feed at about 7a.m. and then muck out. You also want to allow enough time for having your own breakfast, and for making a sandwich to take in your pocket if that is what you like. Otherwise, pop in a chocolate bar, along with a clean handkerchief, a penknife, a cheque or cash for field money or cap, change for the telephone, spare or liner gloves and, if you suffer from chapped lips, a lipsalve, as well as spare hair nets for lady riders. I do not think it very wise to take boiled sweets as there is a danger that you may choke on one.

Grooming

I usually follow feeding by grooming, but there are problems. One is the lack of natural daylight at that time of day, and another is that with a horse that gets excited about going hunting, the activity may put him off his breakfast, especially if you are also plaiting.

Another set-back is the possibility that, having groomed, gone in for breakfast, changed and come back to the stable to tack-up you find your horse has meanwhile rolled! Not only has he now got straw or shavings in his tail, but he has managed to acquire a stable stain too, and the only time you have left is for loading and leaving! So it may be better to groom later, and then leave him tied up.

Tacking Up

Allow more time than you think necessary for tacking up. I always find adjusting a Grakle noseband, for instance, takes longer than I had bargained for. If you own two horses, make sure you have put out the correct-length girth for the one you are taking that day.

Loading

Travel your horse tacked up, and with a top rug secured over. Also take a sweat

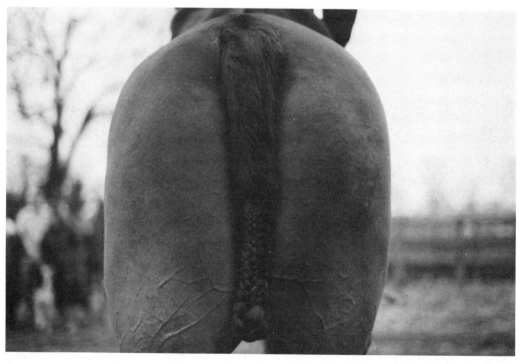

Fig 79 (a)-(c)   Three styles of plaited tail, the third including a red ribbon to warn of a kicker. Plaiting saves the tail from getting very bedraggled and heavy with mud.

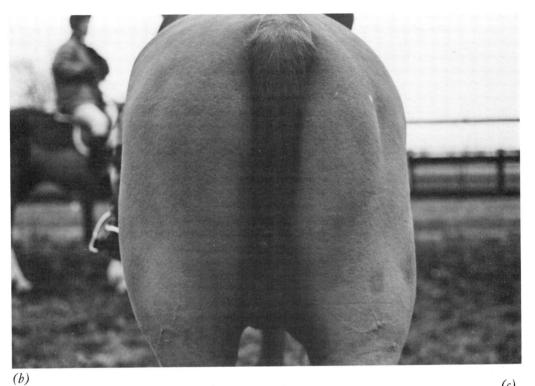

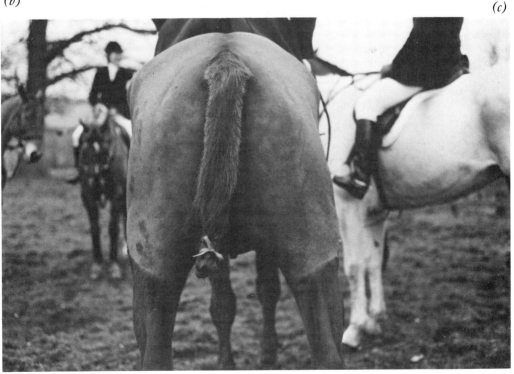

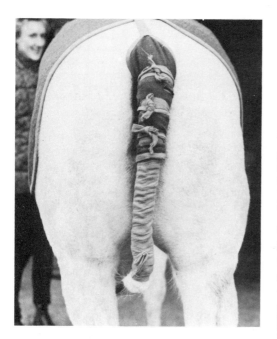

Fig 80 Ready for travelling. The tail bandages will protect the tail from being rubbed raw.

sheet with you to have on under the rug for the return journey. It is sensible also to have on knee pads, leg boots or protectors and a tail bandage or guard. Take a haynet for the return journey and, if you are travelling far, a water container, bucket, sponge and sweat scraper.

Put the head collar on over the bridle and make sure that you attach the rope to breakable twine when you tie the horse up. Do not tie him so short that his head and neck are too restricted.

If you are alone, it is to be hoped that you have already ensured your horse is a good loader. Little is worse than a bad loader, and on your own it is impossible. Both mine walk straight in which is terrific. I then have to perform athletically to nip out of the side door and round

to the back to lift the ramp without the horse trying to come out backwards. If you have breeching straps or chains, you will save a few seconds.

I had just loaded my mare at the end of the day one season when another follower went by at a spanking trot; the mare then pulled back and shot across the road into the adjacent field. Imagine my horror as she then quite gently cantered up the side to be level with the other horse, whose rider kept trotting on. As bad luck would have it, there was another open gate at the far end, so not unnaturally she joined the other horse, the pair of them trotting over the brow of the hill about half a mile distant. All I could do was fasten the ramp and drive off in pursuit, knowing the road over the hill to be slippery. As I arrived there, some kind, non-horsey gentleman was bravely holding my mare, while the other rider had apparently told him the loose horse was nothing to do with him and trotted implacably on!

I must emphasize that this sort of behaviour is exceedingly rare. Most people in the hunting field are only too willing and quick to offer assistance when needed, often sacrificing a good hunt themselves to do so. So remember to go by slowly as someone else is loading, and if they are in difficulties offer to help. Very often, just another presence behind a horse is enough to make him load.

Transport

Travelling by Trailer

When lifting the ramp, unless your trailer is fitted with a tail rope which will keep the horse in place, I advise lifting it from the side. It is easier from the middle, but should the horse run out backwards as you have got the ramp half way up, you will find half a ton of ramp and horse landing on your leg exceedingly painful. It once happened to me and although I had not, as I thought, broken my thigh, the flesh is still dented!

The problem should not occur with a lorry, as there will be tail gates to pull across before the ramp is lifted. Whichever your form of transport, keep the ramp well sprung, especially if you are a lightweight woman on your own!

A trailer should be serviced once a year, preferably in the autumn before the season starts, when you can check it for rust, any weak spots in the floor, the brakes and the ramp springs. The servicing should include checking that the lights work and keeping the hitch and jockey wheel sufficiently oiled.

There is nothing that delights men more than to watch women reversing a trailer, or attempting to. The answer is to practise at home and remember a few basic rules. The most important thing to get into your head is that you must turn the steering wheel in the opposite direction to that which you want to go. Sit for a moment or two and make yourself do this against your natural instinct. The next thing is not to overdo it, or you will find yourself turning the trailer 'inside out' and getting stuck. Turn the steering a little one way and then a little the other.

When it comes to narrow gateways, it is as well to remember this. If you know the trailer can just fit through and you are driving in a straight line, then you only have to watch one side. If you are clearing this by a couple of inches, then it follows that the other side will be cleared, too. You should put the trailer brake hook across for the manoeuvre and unhook it afterwards.

Travel a single horse or the heavier of two horses on the driver's side of the trailer, as this keeps the trailer better balanced towards the crown of the road and not the gutter.

Travelling by Lorry

Needless to say, a lorry should be serviced and maintained in the same way as any other vehicle. It will offer a more comfortable journey to a horse than a trailer, but will cost more in tax, insurance and maintenance. Small boxes such as those that are fitted on to Ford Transit or Bedford CF chassis ought to have heavy-duty rear springs.

A good many lorries are very heavy for women to drive, and lack refinements such as power-assisted steering. However, large lorries, which may only be driven by a Heavy Goods Vehicle licence holder, will have power-assisted steering.

Homeward Bound

What you do at the end of the day depends partly on circumstances, on how far away you are from home and on the state of your horse. If you are lucky enough to be near a stream in which you can wash off, or finish at a farm where the owner is happy to lend you a hose, then so much the better. Otherwise, it is almost certainly a case of travelling straight home as he is. Load him and tie him up so that he cannot turn around, nip out and secure the ramp. Then go back in and take off his saddle and bridle, put the head collar back on again and give him his

Fig 81 *Holding a lead rope correctly. Never wind the loose end around your hand – if the horse pulls suddenly you could suffer severe rope burn or worse.*

haynet. Put on the sweat sheet and over this the top rug. If he is very hot and sweaty, put this on inside out.

A note to remember when leading a horse, either to load or at any other time, is not to wrap the end of the rope or rein around your hand. Should something cause your horse to snatch back suddenly, you may suffer severe and painful rope burn or worse, perhaps torn ligaments. Also, should your horse happen to stand on your foot, do not fall into the trap of saying 'whoa'!

Hacking Home

If you are hacking home, loosen the girth one hole and go at a steady pace. Do not go galloping, and do walk the last mile so that he will be nicely settled and cool when home.

If it is getting dark, try to keep on verges or make sure you can be seen, using your hand to wave down traffic. It is a good idea to carry a reflective arm band in your pocket for those occasions when you find yourself out late and a long way from home or trailer.

Back Home

If your horse is still wet or just damp on your return, I believe the best thing is to hose him down. This is not a universally held view, but I have found no disadvantages to it. When you have finished hosing, get rid of excess water with a sweat scraper and dry his heels and elbows with a towel (to prevent mud fever or cracked heels).

Put on a sweat rug (possibly with straw under it) and take him for a walk, or let him roam in a barn while you get on with other jobs. If you have one with straw in, he will roll and relax, doing himself no end of good. Encourage him to stale, by whistling and rustling the straw. This will also help him relax. Let him have a little water, preferably with the chill taken off it, and prepare a bran mash. Beer in his feed makes a nice pick-me-up after a long day (but try it first on a non-hunting day to check that he likes it.)

Re-stable him, put on at least a top rug and leave him be until later when you will give him his full feed and put on his blankets. Quite often I leave the sweat sheet on all night under the blankets, providing it is dry. If his ears are cold or clammy, give them a nice rub and be friends with him generally. If your horse does not like a mash, just give him a small feed and then a bigger one later.

If when you get him home he is dry, you have to decide whether to wet him again or brush him. To some extent this will depend on how much mud is plastered over him and how ticklish he is. Generally, I favour getting off the worst of the mud, making him comfortable, and then leaving him. Insisting on brushing it all off can lead to him breaking out in a sweat, being put off his feed, and doing more harm than good. Make sure you have checked for cuts and thorns and deal with them, but otherwise it is amazing how much dry mud will have come off by itself come the morning.

The End of the Day

So now you have got back to the house, and you have put on the kettle and, if necessary, the immersion heater. Oh, for that cup of tea, boiled egg and toast, and a hot bath, followed by whisky in front of a roaring log fire among good company!

But what about your dirty boots and tack? Force yourself to wash them off while they are still damp, and you must tree your boots to prevent them from going wrinkly. If they are wet inside, stuff them up to the top with newspaper that night.

The tack should be soaped when it has dried naturally and the polish should go on the boots after drying them with a cloth or chamois leather. The shining can wait, possibly until after a second application of polish. Include your spur straps and whip in this cleaning, and remember to polish the inside of your spur straps to prevent them rubbing off the polish on the boot.

Once you have done all this, it will be time to finish rugging up your horse and give him his final feed. By then you will be pretty hungry yourself, but well satisfied.

10 Injuries and Ailments

Mishaps are inevitable in the hunting field yet, when one considers the unknown terrain that is crossed and the number of hours spent out in the field, it is remarkable that there are not more. Hunters are tough creatures with a strong sense of self-preservation and, once they have hunted for a season or two, unless they are totally unsuited temperamentally, they will anticipate situations.

One of the greatest joys is when they have learnt what the whole thing is about and convey that to you. Their ears prick up at the distant sound of hounds or horn, they suddenly stare, you follow the gaze and there is Charlie himself ...

As a newcomer to hunting, it is as well to be aware of some of the preventable mishaps so that you can avoid them, and to learn what can be done once something has gone wrong.

At Home

Azoturia

Let us begin with a stable management problem, azoturia, also known as set-fast, tying-up, or Monday morning disease. It most often occurs in fit horses who are in fast work and on hard food followed by a day's rest, hence the last nickname.

If the hard food (protein) is not reduced during his day off, or especially during a longer lay off, and he is then set straight off into hard work the next time he is ridden, he may suddenly stiffen up, come to a grinding halt, and be virtually unable to go on. It is very painful for the horse. The muscle cells which are still full of stored food are suddenly being required to provide energy, and the system cannot cope. The muscles tie up or set fast and he is unable to move. The horse will sweat, much as he would with colic, the muscles in the back and hindquarters become hard and painful and he will have a temperature. He may pass, with difficulty, dark, strong-smelling urine.

Veterinary attention at the soonest possible moment is essential. Meanwhile keep the horse warm. When the vet comes the horse will be given cortisone injections and sodium salicylate.

It should go without saying that when recovered, he must not be given too much hard food. Build it up gradually as his exercise is built up again.

For some reason, some horses are more prone to this problem than others, particularly mares. So after hunting on a Saturday, and while you are enjoying a lie in on Sunday, remember the horse must at least be walked out during the day, trotted up to check that he is sound, and must have his hard food reduced.

Influenza and Tetanus

I am including these as a reminder, already mentioned previously on page 22, of the importance of annual vaccination against these diseases. And while you are about it, make sure your own tetanus inoculation is also up to date.

Influenza There was an equine influenza outbreak in the winter of 1989–90 (the first since 1981) due, probably, to lapses in some quarters in vaccinating, although several racehorses, who have to be jabbed annually, also succumbed to it.

Many horsemen are sceptical about flu vaccinations. My big, young mare who had previously had one jab, caught it, and so did my son's newly acquired elderly pony who had almost certainly never had one. Stabled between them and under the same roof was my other hunter who had been vaccinated annually for seven years and he did not get it.

If your horse does get flu or the cough, you must keep him warm and keep the environment dust free. This will mean a bed of paper or shavings instead of straw and hay soaked for twelve to twenty-four hours, with all his feed damped. Some strains will respond to antibiotics, but virus infection will not.

The horse will have a runny nose, be off his feed and run a temperature, much as with a heavy cold or flu in a human. He must be given complete rest, good ventilation, and his hard food must be reduced. Recovery is a matter of taking one day at a time. Sometimes the illness will last five days, sometimes up to two weeks, especially the coughing part.

It is no use hurrying him back to work or he could end up with his wind permanently damaged. Indeed, this is one of the most common causes of respiratory problems, along with Chronic Obstructive Pulmonary Disease. Do not trot at all if there is still a cough at the walk, and if he coughs at the trot, bring him back to the walk for another day or two. On no account do fast work until his lungs are truly clear of infection.

Tetanus As for tetanus, also called lock jaw, this is a ghastly, usually incurable disease in both horses and humans, and certain areas of land are rife with it. The germs live in the soil and an animal can be infected by the germ entering even a small wound. If a horse contracts tetanus, he will become very stiff and then be unable to move. He may eat a little gruel offered to him, but once lying down he is unlikely to rise again. If he does recover, he will do so fully. The simple answer is an annual booster vaccination.

Colic

This is another problem of stable management. Colic is a stomach ache, often acute, causing the horse to sweat, to paw the ground in distress, to keep swinging his head and neck round towards his flank where he is feeling the pain, and roll a lot. Call the vet immediately to prevent the colic becoming acute when twisted gut and death may follow. The vet will give a laxative, antispasmodic drugs and tranquillizers.

Prevention should be possible by: (i) not feeding very new hay, (ii) keeping to regular feeding times to prevent a hungry horse bolting his food, and (iii) not feeding over-dry food.

Chronic Obstructive Pulmonary Disease

One of the facts that has come increasingly to light in the last twenty years is the effect of dust mites on a horse's respiration and consequently on his performance. Chronic Obstructive Pulmonary Disease is also known as COPD and there is something that can be done about it.

Many horses are allergic to hay spores,

dust and fungi. This is shown by a tendency to cough. If allowed to continue like this, the horse will become broken winded, meaning it will be hard for him to breathe at speed, he will 'make a noise', and his value and, more importantly, his performance will be permanently reduced.

The solution is to give him hay that has been soaked for twenty-four hours which causes the spores to swell so much that they cannot pass into the horse's lungs; to give him dust-free bedding, either of shavings or shredded paper; and you must also make sure there is good ventilation in the stable, including a vent in the roof. Also, you must clean the stable before he comes in for the autumn and do not place the muck heap too close to it.

Injuries Out Hunting

The most common injuries suffered out hunting are caused by kicks, treads, stakes, flints, and wire.

Kicks

Try, at all costs, to avoid being kicked out hunting, even if it does mean losing your turn in a queue. Although a habitual kicker is to be frowned upon, it is nevertheless the kicked person who is at fault if they over-ride another horse.

A kick on the forearm, elbow or hock can often cause a star or radius fracture. The horse may seem sound at the time but it is safer to take him home, otherwise when he next jumps or meets uneven ground, the unseen star fracture may turn into a terminal compound fracture. He should not do fast work for ten days.

If the skin has been opened by the kick, the wound must be cleaned and dressed with ointment as soon as possible. Wound powder should only be used on superficial wounds which want drying up, such as grazes. Warm, salted water is best for washing.

If the worst happens, and a horse has clearly broken his leg irreparably, it is quite likely that a member of the hunt staff will carry a humane killer with him and will despatch him. If the horse is insured, it is probably wise to get a vet there first to certify that the action is necessary, but if the horse is in real distress, the sooner he is put out of his misery the better. Until help arrives, immobilize him, and keep him as calm and warm as possible. The hunt kennels will also deal with collecting him and, with CB radios or car telephones now used in a number of hunts, the whole thing may be dealt with very speedily.

To dwell on the subject one moment, when your hunter comes to the end of his days, do the decent thing and call the kennels. To put him down at home, in his familiar surroundings without distress or fuss is the least service you can do for him after all the service he has given you. Abattoirs are strictly controlled and licensed and you would know what happened to him (unlike selling him cheaply at a sale), and they would give you carcass value, but hunting's tradition is to call the kennels, and you will know your horse has not suffered.

Treads and Over-Reaches

A tread is caused by another horse treading on the heels of your horse (and who can blame him if he kicks in protest?), and an over-reach is caused by a hind leg of

111

your horse treading on the heel of his own front leg.

Both cause similar injuries, usually breaking the skin and bruising, and they can be quite sore. If your horse is sound it is probably all right to continue, but when you get home make sure you clean it thoroughly and either put wound powder or cream on it. Some horses are more prone to over-reaching than others due to their action, but deep mud will often also be a cause. In these circumstances it is wise to put on over-reach boots, if you can find a variety that stays in place.

Stake Wounds

A serious stake wound can be one of the worst injuries, especially if a stake has thrust up a horse's chest, and therefore immediate veterinary attention must be sought.

While you are waiting for the vet to come, stop the bleeding and keep the horse still. If a large mass of muscle has been opened, it might be necessary to stuff several handkerchiefs into the wound. Place a jacket over his hindquarters to keep him warm (assuming that there is no foot follower nearby who can provide a blanket), and arrange for transport to be brought as near to the horse as possible.

Smaller stake wounds, probably caused by a sharp, cut stake in a hedge, may not be noticed until you have got back home and, if not seen and dealt with, could become infected. The sort of places where you should look for such a wound are the armpits, the inside thighs, under the belly, on the breast and between the front legs. Clean the affected area thoroughly and dress it.

Lacerations

Do you know how to apply a tourniquet? You may never have to do one, but if a horse is cut on an artery, your knowledge may save his life. You should not be short of the material needed out hunting, as this is where your stock can be used in emergency. If you need to tighten the tourniquet, you can insert a stick in the knot to twist it tighter.

A tourniquet, correctly applied just above the wound, literally blocks the flow of blood. A tourniquet should only be used in exceptionally severe cases of bleeding and must be loosened occasionally to stop the horse going down.

Otherwise, apply pressure on the wound, putting on clean handkerchiefs and holding them firm while someone else keeps the horse still. If the handkerchief becomes soaked in blood, do not remove it, but press more clean ones on top. You can bandage the pads in place by using a stock again.

Get a vet to the horse as soon as possible to stitch the cut. If you have a borderline cut, a stitch or two inserted will often mean the horse will be out of action for less time than if not stitched.

For less serious cuts, you must use your common sense and, if it seems safe to continue, just remember to deal with it at home. It may have become covered over in mud and almost invisible. Check for tell-tale dried blood in amongst the mud and wash or hose it clean, then dress it. If in any doubt, call the vet.

Foot Problems

It is all too easy for your horse to get bruised feet, especially if he is rather flat-footed. Some of the terrain crossed out hunting is very rough and if you go down old railways where flints abound, or over rubble with lots of sharp-edged broken bricks (often found in gateways), you may not be able to avoid trouble. Even if your horse has not gone lame, you must check his feet when you get home. There may be a wedged stone or even a nail, or evidence of a wound.

The best thing to do with a foot wound is to put a bran poultice on it to draw out dirt and poison. Put some dry bran on to a piece of sacking that is big enough to cover the whole foot, then pour boiling water on it. Allow it to cool a little, then put the horse's foot in the middle of the bran, pull up the sacking around the foot and up to the pastern and tie it in place.

Very often the best person to deal with a foot problem is the blacksmith, and it is worthwhile calling him before a vet.

Tendon Strain

A tendon sprain or strain inevitably means at least six months' rest. It is most usual in racehorses when the speed of galloping and/or jumping at racing pace proves too much for the tendon to take, especially as thoroughbred limbs are often fairly fine.

Unfortunately, it can also happen with hunters, even though they usually have greater bone. It can be brought about by poor conformation, through unfitness causing greater strain, or by rough ground or over-galloping, or bad luck such as putting a leg down a rabbit hole (watch out for these when going round the edge of fields by a hedge). A nasty tendon bruise can also be caused by landing too steeply in deep mud and over-reaching higher up the leg, knocking the tendon.

Your horse may not go lame until that evening or even the following morning, but the tell-tale signs will be there – heat and filling. Running your hand down your horse's cannon bones should be a part of daily routine, so that you quickly detect any heat or swelling.

For a strain or sprain, you can poultice the affected part to bring down the swelling and you can cold hose for five minutes every hour or so in the first twenty-four hours to reduce the inflammation. A pressure bandage should be put on the whole way up the leg, and also on the other front leg as that will be carrying more weight than usual to compensate, as the horse will try to ease the weight off his painful leg.

Thorns and Knee Bumps

Part of routine checking when home must include looking for thorns if you have jumped hedges, and looking for bumps on the knee if you know you have hit a solid obstacle such as wall or timber. Thorns should be pulled out, and bumps should be cold hosed.

Mud Fever and Cracked Heels

Akin to chapped hands or lips, mud fever is particularly prone to pale-skinned horses, especially those with white legs. Some soils produce it more than others. Half washing a muddy horse may only succeed in spreading the problem and it can even occur along the belly and flanks, but it is the heels and lower legs where it is usually found. The horse can end up with wide open, painful cracks in his heels, causing swelling and lameness, and bleeding, scabby spots on the legs.

Prevention is better than cure, and one

good idea is to smear petroleum jelly well into the horse's heels before going hunting. The other important way of prevention is never to brush his muddy legs when wet as you will only be rubbing the mud fever in further. Either wash thoroughly and dry, or leave until the morning and brush it off when dry.

A horse with mud fever should have gamgee under bandages to keep the heels warm and dry, having first had them dressed with antiseptic powder and petroleum jelly.

Back Problems

Sometimes when a horse starts refusing uncharacteristically out hunting, it may be that he has put his back out. If he feels one-sided, or if you notice that he is scuffing the toe of one hind shoe and not the other, these are other clues. It is well worth while getting his back checked by your vet or chiropractor who can easily manipulate it back into place and, after only a few days rest, your horse will be transformed back to his old self.

11 The Summer Holiday

After a long season stabled and hunting regularly, your horse must have a holiday in the summer.

He must be allowed that great tonic, Mr Green, but he must **not** be turned straight out without a roughing-off period. His hard food must be reduced slowly, his hay increased (a few hours daily in a paddock picking at the spring grass is ideal), and his rugs must be reduced to toughen him up and adjust to the new routine.

His shoes should be removed, or at least his hind ones, which will reduce the danger to another horse from kicking. If he is to be out for three months, he must have his feet trimmed at least once during that time by the blacksmith. If the ground becomes very hard in a dry summer, you may need to have front shoes at least put

Fig 82   A prize-winning young hunter.

Fig 83 The annual hunter show is the 'shop window' for hunter breeding.

back on, otherwise you may end up with very brittle, broken hooves which will not only cause soreness (like breaking a fingernail below the quick), but will also cause shoeing problems in the autumn.

At grass your horse must be visited daily. If possible he should be turned out with a companion, for horses are herd animals, and also two together can stand head to tail in the heat and switch flies off each other's faces.

Unfortunately no end of mishaps can and do occur at grass, and daily inspection is imperative. Watch out for broken fencing, barbed or even plain wire and discarded litter. There is always the possibility of kicks and bites; I never have sexes mixed unevenly at grass. A mare

Fig 84 The hunter at summer grass. Note the freeze brand identification, a safety measure against theft.

116

Fig 85   Peterborough Royal Foxhound Show, the high-spot of the summer in hunting circles.

and gelding are fine, or two of each, but one of one sex and two of the other is not a good idea.

A problem which may beset pale-skinned horses is sweet-itch. This is an allergy to midges, causing the horse to rub his neck and dock so hard that they become open and sore. One remedy is to stable the horse for an hour or two at dawn and dusk when the midges are prevalent. Otherwise, a daily application of a Benzyl Benzoate lotion should ease the itching. In very severe cases, a long-lasting injection can be given by the vet.

A pale-skinned horse can also suffer from sunburn. Shade and shelter are important for all horses turned out.

Ponies are inclined towards laminitis if allowed too much rich grass, but hunters, also, can get it and should not be allowed to get overweight. Also, if they are too fat, there can be quite a problem getting them fit in the autumn and the fat can cause a degeneration of the liver. One final thing, do not forget your worming routine, which is especially important at grass when the land may be infested with worms.

117

12 Supporters' Clubs and Car Followers

Since the late Dorian Williams founded the Whaddon Chasers in about 1955, supporters' clubs have grown and flourished throughout hunting. Indeed, many packs today would be in financial difficulty without them. They are great for fund-raising, great for socializing (the two often going together; if funds have to be raised they may as well be raised while people are enjoying themselves) and great for all walks of life rubbing shoulders together – as, indeed, is hunting as a whole.

Many foot and car followers will join the supporters' club and in some areas a small fee or 'car cap' will be taken. For them, there is not the ride, but there is still the thrill of the chase, and although car followers are often grumbled at for heading the fox, their enthusiasm has to be admired.

If they can manage not to line a road so densely that a fox heading their way is not inevitably turned, so much the better. And, as with a mounted follower, they must not holloa in the face of a fox, thus

Fig 86   A hunt fund-raising event.

Fig 87   Car followers. It can be difficult for the fox to cross a
road lined with cars.

Fig 88   The flesh wagon. One of the services the hunt gives is
the collection of fallen stock from local farmers. This provides
the chief source of meat for the hounds.

Fig 89   Team chasing is also hunting-related.

heading him, but wait until he is well on his way first. They should also switch off their car engines, not only to reduce noise but also to stop smelly fumes which will put hounds off the fox's scent.

These non-subscribing followers are often prepared to dip deep into their pockets in order to help the hunt. A good few hunts boast special hound trailers, new horse-boxes or even horses, repairs to hunt properties and a wide variety of other expensive items, thanks to their supporters. Social and fund-raising functions will include pub events such as skittles, darts and inter-hunt quizzes; supporters' dances; terrier shows and racing; putting on hunt entertainments such as pantomimes, auctions, and so

forth. Newsletters or hunt magazines are also increasing and are another way of promoting goodwill and happy public relations within the farming and hunting fraternity.

The Melton Hunt Club

Before you know where you are, autumn will be approaching, and you will be looking forward to renewing acquaintances with your new-found hunting friends and, especially, with your hunter. By now, after your first season, you are sure to be a full subscriber to your local pack. You will be joining in social events, and you will belong to the British Fields

Sports Society, which safeguards the interests and future of all field sportsmen.

You may also, in your new-found enthusiasm, wish to sample a little hunting in some of the more fashionable areas, and where better than in the shires, rightly famed throughout the world as the cream of the cream in fox-hunting for two hundred years.

In order to obtain a coveted day with either the Quorn (pronounced Kworn), the Belvoir (Beever) or the Cottesmore (Cotsmore), it will be necessary to join the Melton Hunt Club, founded in 1956

by the late Lance Newton and admirably carried on since his death by the Hon. Ursula Newton, in whose capable hands the Club continues to flourish.

Founded to help promote the co-existence of hunting and farming in the shires, it does tremendous groundwork in those countries, as well as providing its members with an annual chance to hunt there. It also runs one of the most prestigious point-to-points at Garthorpe, near Melton Mowbray, 'capital' of the shires, on which country town three packs converge. There is a membership

Fig 90   Capt. Brian Fanshawe MFH jumping timber in Leicestershire with the Cottesmore Hunt, one of the three shire hunts in the Melton Hunt Club scheme.

121

Fig 91　The hunt's annual point-to-point sometimes succumbs
to the weather.

Fig 92　The runners stream over the first fence, all of them
having qualified to point-to-point in the hunting field.

fee which entitles members to two days' hunting, each day with a different pack, at a reduced cap during the season, (but not with the Quorn for first-season members). It is up to members to book their days well in advance to be sure of getting their allotted days. There are some 1,500 members and the hunts only allow certain numbers out each day.

The Club also holds an annual cross-country ride which, in some respects, is like an old-fashioned point-to-point over about three and a half miles of natural country. There is also a sponsored ride and various other fund-raising functions.

From the funds, each of the three host hunts receive an annual donation and a further amount for improving their country, including hedge-cutting grants.

Donations are also made to the BFSS, the Hunt Servants Benefit Society, local Pony Club branches and various local charities, so it can be seen that the Club is of great mutual benefit to the shire hunts, Melton Hunt Club members and the countryside alike.

It is to be hoped that by now your appetite has been sufficiently whetted to start you on a life-long love affair with hunting. Who knows, the next thing you will be wanting to try, in conjunction with it, is point-to-pointing, but then that sport must be left to another book. Finally, do not be afraid to ask an old timer anything at all about hunting – he or she will be only too pleased to pass on his or her fund of knowledge.

Useful Addresses

Baily's Hunting Directory
J. A. Allen & Co. Ltd.,
The Horseman's Bookshop,
1 Lower Grosvenor Place,
Buckingham Palace Road,
London, SW1W OEL
Tel: (071) 834 0090

British Field Sports Society
59 Kennington Road,
London, SE1 7PZ
Tel: (071) 928 4742

Horse and Hound
Editor, Michael Clayton,
King's Reach Tower,
Stamford Street,
London, SE1 9LS
Tel: (071) 261 5000/6315

Hounds Magazine
Editor, Michael Sagar,
Rose Cottage,
Hughley,
Shrewsbury,
Salop
Tel: (074636) 637

Hunt Servants Benefit Society
Anthony Hart,
Parsloes Cottage,
Bagendon,
Cirencester,
Glos., GL7 7DU
Tel: (0285) 83470

Irish Masters of Foxhounds Association
Secretary, Robin de Vere Hunt,
Rockmount,
Kilmacthomas,
Co. Waterford
Tel: (051) 91183

Masters of Foxhounds Association
Secretary, Anthony Hart, (*see under* Hunt Servants Benefit Society)
Public Relations Officer, Brian Toon,
46a Castle Street,
Hinckley,
Leics., LE10 1DD
Tel: (0455) 613143

Melton Hunt Club
Hon. Mrs U. Newton,
Church Farm,
Saltby,
Melton Mowbray,
Leics.
Tel: (0476) 860240

The Pony Club; The British Horse Society
British Equestrian Centre,
Stoneleigh,
Kenilworth,
Warwickshire, CV8 2LR
Tel: (0203) 696697

New Zealand

New Zealand Hunts' Association
Secretary, Mr H.J. Poland,
PO Box 11241,
Wellington 1

USA

**Master of Foxhounds Association
of America**
Clerk and Keeper of the Stud Book,
Mr John B. Glass,
294 Washington Street,
Room 851,
Boston, Mass.

Further Reading

Aldin, Cecil, *Ratcatcher to Scarlet* (Eyre & Spottiswoode Ltd., 1932)

Clayton, Michael, *The Chase: A Modern Guide to Foxhunting* (Stanley Paul, 1987)

Jackson, Alastair, *Hunting* (Pony Club Publications, 1988)

Rossdale, Peter D. and Wreford, Susan M., *The Horse's Health from A to Z* (David and Charles, 1974)

Summerhays, R. S., *Encyclopaedia for Horsemen* (Frederick Warne & Co., 1952)

Watson, J. N. P., *A Concise Guide to Hunting* (The Sportsman's Press, 1988)

Index